CHARMING S

GREECE

CHARMING SMALL HOTEL GUIDES

GREECE

EDITED BY

Robin Gauldie

DUNCAN PETERSEN

This first edition
conceived, designed and produced by
Duncan Petersen Publishing Ltd,
31 Ceylon Road, London W14 0PY

Editorial Director Andrew Duncan
Editor Robin Gauldie
Production Editor Nicola Davies
Art Editor Don Macpherson
Production Sarah Hinks
Maps Eugene Fleury
The author has asserted his moral right

Published 2002 by
Duncan Petersen Publishing Ltd,
31 Ceylon Road, London W14 0PY

Sales representation and distribution in the U.K. and Ireland by
Portfolio Books Limited
Unit 5, Perivale Industrial Park
Horsenden Lane South
Greenford, UB6 7RL
Tel: 0208 997 9000 Fax: 0208 997 9097
E-mail: sales@portfoliobooks.com

A CIP catalogue record for this book is available
from the British Library

ISBN 1-903301-21-1

Published in the USA by
Hunter Publishing Inc.,
130 Campus Drive, Edison, N.J. 08818.
Tel (732) 225 1900 Fax (732) 417 0482

For details on hundreds of other travel guides and language courses, visit
Hunter's Web site at http://www.hunterpublishing.com

ISBN 1-58843-291-2

DTP by Duncan Petersen Publishing Ltd
Printed by G. Canale & C., Italy

Contents

INTRODUCTION

IN THIS INTRODUCTORY SECTION

Homeric Poems, Santorini, Southern Aegean

Welcome to this first edition of the Charming Small Hotel Guide to Greece. It's some years since we began wondering if we could publish this guide: Greece was for so long a country of big, soulless package holiday hotels, or small 'village rooms' built to the specifications of international tour operators, all of which were open only from May to mid-October.

But things have changed in Greece during the last five years, which is why we now add this guide to the series. It is the only English language publication of its kind. Since the early 1990s, a quiet revolution has been taking place in the Greek hotel world.

Quiet, because few foreign visitors and still fewer guidebooks have taken notice of a new kind of hotel on Greece's islands and mainland which you will find in this guide. Scores of charming old buildings have been rescued from dilapidation and restored to become small hotels and guesthouses with real character, often enthusiastically run by members of families which have owned them for generations. These are the mainstay of this guide, often with added charm because Greece's vernacular architecture is perhaps the most varied in Europe, enriched by both historic and geographical influences.

On Crete and Corfu, you'll find them in stylish town house hotels in old Venetian mansions. On Santorini, traditional cave houses built on the lip of a sea-filled volcanic crater have become uniquely colourful places to stay. On Mikonos, hotels in old Cycladic village houses, or built with due deference to island style, are the epitome of designer chic. On the mainland you can now stay in the miniature castles of the Mani, the beautiful old mansions of the Pilion peninsula, or the sturdy, stone-roofed village houses of the Zagorochoria, high in the Pindos mountains.

Unlike the internationalized, bland properties catering to the mass holiday trade, these hotels are truly Greek, with a mainly Greek clientele. Most stay open all year round, making them great places to stay in spring and autumn as well as during the summer peak season. And out of peak season, you might well benefit from more personal, less hurried service.

Visit charmingsmallhotels.co.uk
Our website has expanded enormously since its launch in early 2001 and continues to grow. It's the best research tool on the web for our kind of hotel.

Exchange rates
As we went to press, $1 bought 0.89 Euros and £1 bought 1.62 Euros.

OUR CRITERIA

Our selection criteria are essentially the same in Greece as they are anywhere. We aim to include places that have charm, real character and (ideally) truly personal service.

While selecting our hotels with great care, we also give a broad range of recommendations to suit all budgets. In the most popular and (in our view) the most attractive islands and regions of Greece, hotels may be fully booked at peak times, and we have included several alternatives. For a detailed summary of our selection criteria, see page 9.

In Greece, as elsewhere in Europe, we have found many properties which met our highly selective approach, but there are some which, although recommendable as the best place to stay in their areas, are not quite perfectly in tune with our criteria. We make this clear in the description of each hotel, but each hotel in this guide is in some way (or ways) true to the ideal of the charming small hotel. If you discover any more, please let us know.

Our readers have many different requirements, and we have been careful to bear this in mind. Some of the places we have selected will fall within even the smallest holiday budget. Others are true luxury hotels with a price tag to match. Most are in between, and affordable to the majority of travellers to Greece.

In order to feature a worthwhile selection of more than two hundred places to stay in Greece, we have included many places that are far from being full-service hotels, but nonetheless worth their place in the guide.

In some, service is casual (one might even say lackadaisical) and is limited to a part-time reception desk, daily room cleaning, linen and towel change. A few are virtually self catering, and many serve only breakfast, snacks, and a limited range of drinks. In almost all, finding a member of staff between midday and early evening (the Greek siesta) can be a challenge. That said, the bar and restaurant facilities that you might have expected to find within your hotel will certainly be available in independent establishments on the same street, sometimes within the same building and frequently run by the same family as your hotel.

Charming and small

Ideally, our recommendations have fewer than 30 bedrooms, but this is not a rigid rule. Some hotels with more than 30 bedrooms feel much smaller, and you will find several such places in this guide. We attach more importance to size than other guides because we feel that unless a hotel is small, it cannot give a genuinely personal welcome. In this guide, however, you will find a handful of larger, resort style hotels. We have included these because of their location, flair and world-class standards, and have selected those which, despite their size, offer a personal welcome and a warm atmosphere.

We think that we have a clearer idea than other guides of what is special and what is not: and we think that we apply these criteria more consistently than other guides because we are a small and personally managed company rather than a bureaucracy. We have a small team of like-minded inspectors, thoroughly rehearsed in recognizing what we want. We very much appreciate

---

So what exactly do we look for? –

- *A peaceful, attractive setting in an interesting and picturesque position.*

- *A building that is either handsome or interesting or historic, or at least with a distinct character.*

- *Bedrooms that are well proportioned with as much character as the public rooms below.*

- *Ideally, we look for adequate space, but on a human scale: we don't go for places that rely on grandeur, or that have pretensions that could intimidate.*

- *Decorations must be harmonious and in good taste, and the furnishings and facilities comfortable and well maintained. We like to see interesting antique furniture that is there because it can be used, not simply revered.*

- *The proprietors and staff need to be dedicated and thoughtful, offering a personal welcome, without being intrusive. The guest needs to feel like an individual.*

readers' reports (see page 14) but they are not our main source of information.

Whole-page entries

We rarely find places to stay which combine all these qualities, but our warmest recommendations – whole-page, with photograph – usually fall only a few points short of the ideal.

Half-page entries

Don't, however, ignore our half-page entries. They are useful addresses, and are all charming small hotels. You can't have stars on every page.

Restaurants

As a new departure for the series, we include in this guide, a sprinkling of restaurants. Many have been selected as much for their location and friendliness as for their menu, but all offer some of the best of Greek traditional cooking, sometimes with a fresh, international twist.

No fear or favour

Unlike many guides, there is no payment for inclusion. The selection is made entirely independently.

How to find an entry

In this guide, the entries are arranged in sections by geographical region, by island group, such as the Cyclades, and by single large island, such as Crete. Within each section, hotels are generally organized alphabetically by city, town or nearest village. If several occur, in or near one town, entries are arranged in alphabetical order by name of hotel.

To find a hotel in a particular area, simply browse through headings at the top of the pages until you find that area – or use the maps following this introduction to locate the appropriate pages.

To locate a specific hotel whose name you know, or a hotel in a specific place, use the indexes at the back, which list the entries alphabetically, first by name and then by place name.

How to read an entry
At the top of each entry is a coloured bar highlighting the place, followed by a categorization which gives some clue to its character. These categories are, as far as possible, self-explanatory.

Fact boxes
The fact box given for each hotel follows a standard pattern: the explanation that follows is for full- and half-page entries.

Tel and Fax The first part of the number given in our entries is the area code within Greece. When calling from the UK dial 00 30; from the US, 001 30; then the full number.

E-mail Many Greek hotels and guesthouses now use e-mail, which is a quick and efficient way to find, book and confirm **Websites** are listed when available

Location
The location and setting of the hotel are briefly described and any useful information included to help you find your way there. Where parking is provided or available, we have made a note.

Food Under this heading we list meals available on the premises. Many of the hotels listed also offer basic self-catering facilities in bedrooms. If in doubt, check in advance with the selected hotel.

Prices We use price bands rather than figures:

€	less than 20 euros
€€	less than 40 euros
€€€	less than 80 euros
€€€€	80-150 euros
€€€€€	more than 150 euros

For hotels we normally give the range of prices you can expect to pay for a room, including tax and service. Wherever possible we have given prices for the year of publication, but prices may be higher than those quoted because of inflation or other considerations. The Greek government sets a maximum price per room each year for each category of accommodation (hotels, classed A-E, and guesthouses, also classed A-E) but prices may be substantially lower than the maximum permitted. A 10 per cent discount is often offered for stays of more than three nights, even in high season.

For restaurants, we give the approximate price of a meal for two

(starter, main course, salad, and one bottle of wine), but obviously the cost of your food will depend on what you choose, so these prices should be taken only as an indication.

€   less than 30 euros
€€   30-60 euros
€€€   more than 60 euros

Half board is never obligatory in Greek hotels, and not all serve even breakfast. Those which do not will always have basic self-catering facilities, either en suite or shared, so you can prepare your own breakfast. Greek breakfast is usually very simple (coffee, bread and jam or honey, perhaps juice and an egg), and the Greek version of 'English breakfast' bears only a passing resemblance to the real thing.

Rooms Under this heading we indicate the number and type of room – and whether the rooms have baths (usually with shower or shower attachment as well) or just showers.

Facilities Under facilities we list: public rooms, lift, courtyard, garden, terrace or sitting-out area; outdoor or indoor swimming pool; tennis court; sauna, steam room, and fitness facilities.

Credit cards We use the following abbreviations:
    AE   American Express
    DC   Diners Club
    MC   MasterCard (Access)
    V   Visa (Barclaycard/Bank Americard)

Children Children are welcome almost everywhere in Greece. We have, however, made a distinction between children being 'welcome' and being 'accepted'. Some hotels have guests who are mainly child-free couples who have come for peace and quiet. We have also listed a few hotels which we feel are 'not suitable' for children, mainly because they are in urban locations, lack gardens or pools, and offer little to keep children happy and entertained.

Disabled Greece is problematic for people with disabilities. Few small hotels are accessible by wheelchair, and even when it is possible to enter the ground floor and public areas by wheelchair, bed-

rooms are usually at the top of stairs. A few hotels have accessible ground-floor bedrooms, but these may not have specially adapted bathrooms or WCs.

Pets Most Greek hotels (with the exception of some city properties) accept pet dogs, but reserve the right to bar larger, more boisterous pets. Check directly with your hotel.

Closed Many hotels in the islands close from late October until Easter or even May. The dates we have given are those supplied to us by the hotel or guesthouse.

The final entry in the fact box is the name of the proprietor, manager or operating company or organization.

FOR FIRST-TIME VISITORS TO GREECE

First-time visitors to Greece, especially in smaller, cheaper hotels and guesthouses, are often surprised by the following:

- In many places, lavatory paper, tampons and sanitary towels must be disposed of not in the W.C. but in a separate bin (this is emptied at least daily).

- Facecloths and tissues are not provided as standard items.

- Most smaller hotels and guesthouses do not have porters, desk clerks, or even a fully staffed reception. If you need to leave early next morning, it is best to settle your bill the evening before departure.

- Many establishments do not accept credit cards and cash is the preferred means of paying your bill.

REPORTING TO THE GUIDE

Please write and tell us about your experiences of small
hotels, guest houses and inns, whether good or bad, whether
listed in this edition or not. As well as hotels in Greece, we
are interested in hotels in France, Spain, Italy, Austria,
Germany, Switzerland and the U.S.A. We assume that
reporters have no objections to our publishing their views
unpaid.

Readers whose reports prove particularly helpful may be
invited to join our Travellers' Panel. Members give us notice
of their own travel plans; we suggest hotels that they might
inspect, and help with the cost of accommodation.

The address is:

Editor, *Charming Small Hotel Guides*
Duncan Petersen Publishing Limited,
31 Ceylon Road,
London W14 0PY.

Checklist
Please use a separate sheet of paper for each report; include
your name, address and telephone number on each report.

Your reports will be received with particular pleasure if
they are typed, and if they are organized under the following
headings:

Name of establishment
Town or village it is in, or nearest
Full address, including postcode
Telephone number
Time and duration of visit
The building and setting
The public rooms
The bedrooms and bathrooms
Physical comfort (chairs, beds, heat, light, hot water)
Standards of maintenance and housekeeping
Atmosphere, welcome and service
Food
Value for money

We assume that in writing you have no objections to your
views being published unpaid, either verbatim or in an
edited version. Names of major outside contributors are
acknowledged, at the editor's discretion, in the guide.

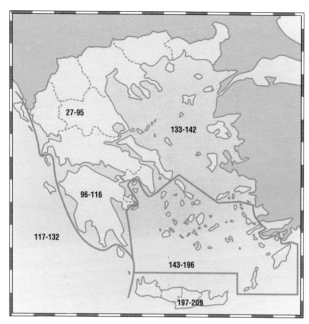

GREEK PLACE NAMES

Greek has its own alphabet, so transliterating place names can be tricky – especially as there is no universally accepted 'correct' system and many place names can be spelt in three or four ways in the Roman alphabet. Chania, for example, can also be referred to as Hania or Xania, Delphi as Delfi or even Delphoi. On main roads, all road signs are in Roman as well as in Greek characters – but any given destination may be spelt several different ways within a few kilometres! In the islands, the main town or village may appear on some maps by the same name as the island (examples are Rhodes and Corfu). On smaller islands it is often also referred to as Chora ('the village'). In this book we have tried to take a consistent but common sense approach to transliterating place names, while also using those variants which are most commonly accepted in Greece. Where well-known English versions of Greek names exist – such as Athens rather than Athinai, Crete rather than Kriti, Attica rather than Attiki – we have preferred these. Elsewhere, we have used the most easily recognized version. In the case of individual properties, we have used the version favoured by the hotel or guest-house owner in signage and brochures. For example, the word 'archontiko' (meaning 'manor' or 'mansion') can also be written 'arxontiko' or 'arhondiko'. If this sounds intimidating, don't worry. Common sense will see you through.

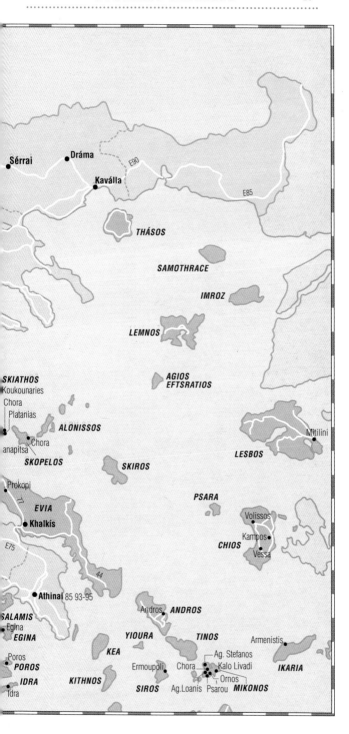

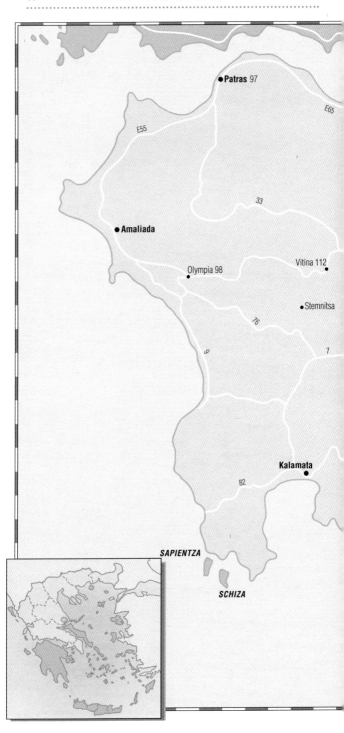

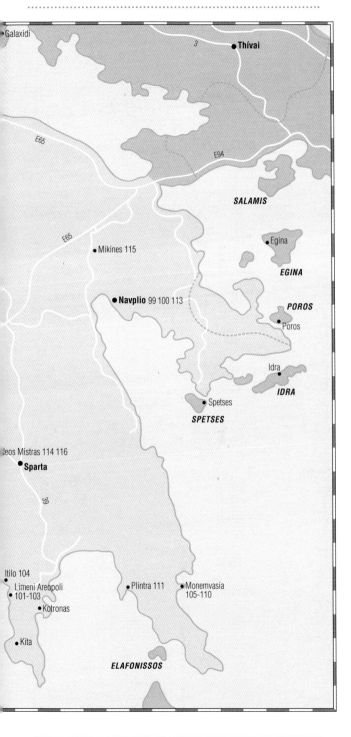

Galaxidi

Thívai

3

E65

E94

SALAMIS

E65

Egina

Mikines 115

EGINA

POROS

Navplio 99 100 113

Poros

Idra

IDRA

Spetses

SPETSES

Jeos Mistras 114 116

Sparta

39

Itilo 104

Limeni Areopoli
101-103

Plintra 111

Monemvasia
105-110

Kotronas

Kita

ELAFONISSOS

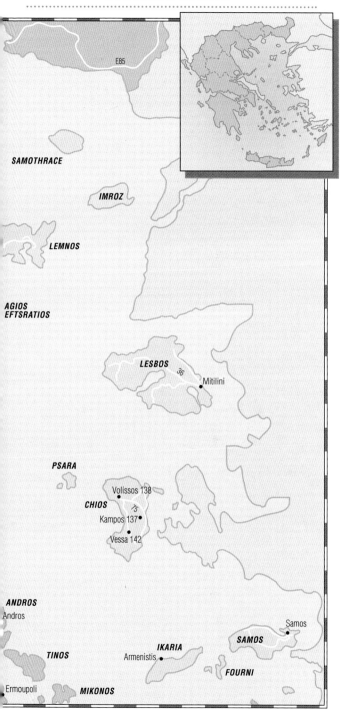

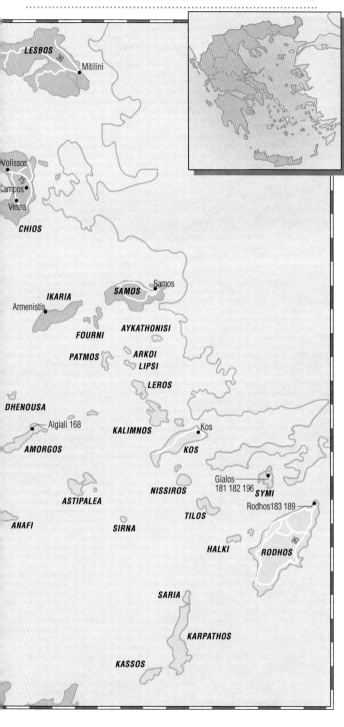

LESBOS
36
Mitilini

Volissos
73
Kampos
Vessa
CHIOS

IKARIA
Armenistis

SAMOS
Samos

AYKATHONISI

FOURNI

PATMOS
ARKOI
LIPSI

LEROS

DHENOUSA

Aigiali 168

KALIMNOS
Kos

AMORGOS
KOS

NISSIROS
Gialos
181 182 196 SYMI
Rodhos183 189

ASTIPALEA

TILOS

ANAFI
SIRNA
HALKI
RODHOS
96

SARIA

KARPATHOS

KASSOS

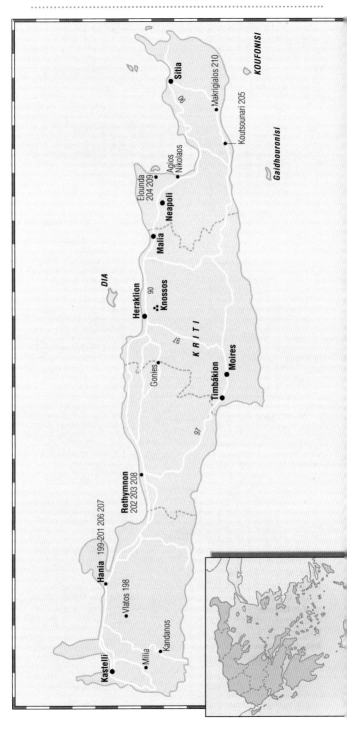

Northern Mainland

The northern mainland comprises all of Greece from the Gulf of Corinth (which separates it from the southern mainland) to the borders of Albania, the former Yugoslav republic of Macedonia, Bulgaria and Turkey, and from the coast of the Ionian Sea in the west to the shores of the Aegean in the east.

It embraces Greece's capital, Athens, a sprawling conurbation which is home to half the country's population, as well as its second largest city, Thessaloniki. There are international, scheduled and charter flights to both of these, as well as less frequent summer charter flights to Preveza, on the west coast, and Volos, on the east. For a tour of the northwest, you could also fly charter to Corfu, a 40-minute hydrofoil ride from the mainland port of Igoumenitsa, which also has overnight ferries from Italy.

The north's landscapes range from rolling plains and farmland to lushly wooded slopes and barren peaks, and on both coasts there are long sandy beaches as well as tiny pebbly bays. Here too are Greece's highest summit, Mt Olympus, its largest lake and its longest river.

The north is also a region of climatic extremes. Mainland Europe's highest summer temperatures have been recorded at Larisa, in Thessaly, while the winter snows which make skiing possible on the slopes of Parnassos and Pilion may linger on the highest summits of Olympus until May or even June.

Reflecting this variety of landscapes and microclimates is a rich vernacular architecture, and in recent years many delightful traditional buildings have been converted into charming small hotels. They include elegant half-timbered apple farmers' mansions in the Pilion villages, stylish old shipowners' houses in villages such as Galaxidi, and sturdy stone cottages in Zagoria, high in the Pindos mountains. As well as these, there are more modern hotels, built of local materials and with at least a nod to regional architectural traditions.

Most of these hotels would lend themselves well to a touring holiday with a hired car, though there are plenty of places which would be perfect for a longer stay. Especially in inland locations, most of their clients are Greek weekenders from Athens, which means that (unlike many hotels in the islands) they stay open year round. It also means that we strongly recommend booking ahead if you plan to visit at a weekend or during the peak Greek holiday times, Easter and August.

Some of the hotels listed in this chapter are in lovely coastal villages, others in mountain and lakeside regions. Greece's two major cities are sadly lacking in small hotels of character (though they have plenty of large international chain properties and bland three-star hotels). In Athens and in Thessaloniki, we have selected properties that come closest to meeting our criteria in a range of budgets from small to generous. Few, it must be admitted, truly deserve full marks, but all are acceptable places to spend a night or two on arrival, before departure, or while seeing the sights.

The northern mainland can be visited year round, and Athens is best seen in late autumn and early winter. Most visitors will want to avoid the cold, wet and windy months of January and February, but March can be a good time for touring and sightseeing. Unlike many hotels in the south, most traditional buildings in the north are built for comfort in cooler weather as well as in summer.

FLORINA

NIMFEO

TA LINOURIA
~ VILLAGE INN ~

53078 Nimfeo, Florina
TEL 031 287626 **FAX** 031 287401

REMINISCENT OF A RANCH HOUSE IN STYLE, Ta Linouria is an attractive stone building which would be even prettier if it had a traditional stone-slabbed roof instead of the rather ugly composite used to replace it. Minor design quibbles aside, this would be an ideal place for a large family or a group of friends, with its eight-bunk and four-bunk rooms. It's less suitable for couples, with only one double room, so book early if you want privacy. Just outside Nimfeo village, it stands amid fields that are green in spring and autumn, less so in summer.

Friendly and informal, it has an attractive coffee-shop restaurant (with tables and chairs outside in summer), which serves Greek-style breakfast (great yoghurt) as well as tasty *meze* to accompany a glass of ouzo or wine, and more substantial locally-made pies. After a day's walking, the home-made puddings are welcome, too.

The interior and the rooms are simply but tastefully furnished and Ta Linouria is well kept by its friendly local staff, but this is a place for those who like the simple outdoor life and are not looking for five-star service or sophisticated wining and dining.

~

NEARBY Lake Kastoria; Prespa lakes; Arcturus bear sanctuary.
LOCATION at entrance to Nimfeo village
FOOD breakfast, lunch, dinner
PRICE ©
ROOMS 2 eight-bunk, 3 four-bunk, 1 twin, all with en suite bath
FACILITIES café-restaurant, souvenir shop
CREDIT CARDS not accepted
CHILDREN welcome
DISABLED access difficult
PETS accepted
CLOSED never
PROPRIETORS Ta Linouria SA

FLORINA

NIMFEO

LA MOARA

~ COUNTRY HOTEL ~

53078 Nimfeo, Florina
TEL 031 287626 **FAX** 031 287401

THIS SOLID LOOKING, three-storey, grey stone mansion set among green lawns and surrounded by mountain scenery is unique in Greece, with something of the flavour of an English country house – there is even a billiards room. La Moara means 'watermill' in the local Vlach language, and the inn was built on the site of an old mill, whose stream still burbles through the grounds. Opened in 1992, it has been designed in the style of the region. Inside, fleecy *flokati* rugs and wooden furniture complement simple whitewashed walls and polished wood floors.

Hostess Erasmia Tsipou oversees preparation of dinner, which is served in a fine dining room with a grand view out on to the slopes of nearby Mt Siniatsiko. This is a cosy place in which to stay, with a warm personal touch and service well above the norm, and with only eight bedrooms the atmosphere is more like that of a private house party than a hotel. It also has perhpas the best cellar in Greece, with 130 wines. Each room has modern en suite bathroom, and La Moara also has a library, TV and video room (though the titles available are limited). Mountain bikes and horses can be hired.

~

NEARBY Lake Kastoria; Prespa lakes; Arcturus bear sanctuary
LOCATION at entrance to Nimfeo village
FOOD breakfast, dinner
PRICE €€€€
ROOMS 8 double, with bath; all rooms have TV, phone, central heating
FACILITIES TV and video room, library, bar, restaurant, cycling, riding
CREDIT CARDS AE, DC, V
CHILDREN welcome
DISABLED not suitable
PETS accepted
CLOSED Sun and Mon
PROPRIETORS Western Macedonian Inns, director Mrs Fani Boutari

KONITSA

BOURAZANI PARK

HOTEL BOURAZANI
~ FOREST LODGE ~

44100 Bourazani, Konitsa
TEL 0655 61320 **FAX** 0655 61321

WELL OFF THE BEATEN TRACK though it is, this really is a place not to miss, well worth the detour. The Hotel Bourazani would qualify for an entry on the strength of its surroundings alone, standing as it does among lush, almost tropical forests of plane and chestnut trees beside one of Greece's loveliest rivers. Its comfortable rooms and good restaurant (with a menu which features wild boar and other game in season) are an unexpected and welcome bonus.

You might almost think yourself at a private safari lodge in Africa, as the hotel is surrounded by a 120,000 square metre private park, close to the splendid Aoos National Park and on the banks of the ice-blue Aoos River. And it even operates its own guided photo-safaris, which take about two and a half hours, during which you can see deer, mouflon and the rare Cretan *kri-kri*.

Originally pasture land belonging to the Tassou family, who still run the park and hotel, Bourazani became first a game reserve, then a private environmental park. Rooms are large and light, with simple decoration, big floor-to-ceiling windows and polished wood floors, and a separate coffee table and seating area.

~

NEARBY Vikos Gorge; Aoos National Park; Mt Timfi; Mt Smolikas.
LOCATION 60 km N of Ioanina; car parking
FOOD breakfast, lunch, dinner
PRICE €€
ROOMS 20 twin with bath; all rooms have TV, radio
FACILITIES private wildlife park, photo-safaris
CREDIT CARDS MC, V
CHILDREN welcome
DISABLED access possible
PETS not accepted
CLOSED never
PROPRIETORS Dimitris and Athanasia Tassos

MACEDONIA

THESSALONIKI

CAPSIS BRISTOL HOTEL

⌁ TOWN HOTEL ⌁

2 Oplopiou & Katouni Street, 54625 Thessaloniki
TEL 031 506500 **FAX** 031 515777
WEBSITE www.capsis.gr

THE NEW IN-PLACE in Thessaloniki is the Capsis Bristol Hotel, in the trendy Ladadika district. Thessaloniki has been long overdue for a small hotel of character, and the Capsis, a new hotel from one of Greece's leading luxury lodging chains, meets this need admirably. Located at the edge of Ladadika's traffic-free block of bars, restaurants and clubs, this is an elegantly restored neoclassical building, built and decorated in a style that reflects the city's historic architecture. The exterior is painted creamy pink and white, with attractive period stucco details. Inside are 16 light, attractive rooms and four larger suites each with a small sitting room. Polished wood plank floors and handmade rugs in traditional patterns from northern Greece give each room an individual touch, and tall windows open on to wrought-iron balconies, so the rooms are light and airy. Downstairs, white canvas umbrellas shade the tables of a pavement café, the perfect place for breakfast in summer, and the hotel also has one of Thessaloniki's better à la carte restaurants, with excellent seafood and a menu that will be a revelation to those who have not sampled the typical dishes of the north. It only lacks a pool, but guests can use the rooftop pool of the Capsis Thessaloniki Hotel, only ten minutes' walk away.

⌁

NEARBY Archaeological Museum; Museum of Byzantine Culture; Byzantine fortress; Halkidiki beaches; Mt Athos; Vergina and Pella archaeological sites.
LOCATION city centre, 25 minutes from airport
FOOD breakfast, lunch, dinner
PRICE €€€€
ROOMS 20; 16 twin, 4 suites, all with bath; all with phone, TV, air conditioning
FACILITIES café-bar, restaurant, breakfast room, lobby lounge, lift
CREDIT CARDS AE, DC, MC, V
CHILDREN accepted
DISABLED access possible
PETS accepted **CLOSED** never
PROPRIETORS Capsis Hotels & Resorts

GREVENA

VASSILITSA

CASA LA MUNDI
∼ COUNTRY RESORT ∼

51100 Vassilitsa, Grevena
TEL 0462 25555 **FAX** 0462 28137

STANDING ALONE IN PASTURELAND on a hillside miles from anywhere, in the backwoods of Grevena province, the Casa la Mundi is a base for a huge range of summer and winter mountain activities ranging from shooting to kayaking and riding.

Ringed by hills, there are sweeping views from the dining room – which is built in the shape of an octagon with picture windows on all sides – and from all the rooms. The building is modern, low rise, and with a nod in the direction of traditional architecture, it could be a ski lodge in any European mountain resort.

Each room has a balcony, and all are modern and comfortable, with thick carpets, soft lighting and warm quilts on the beds. The lobby sitting area, with its dark wooden floors, card tables and dark leather chairs, is definitely clubby, and the restaurant is a welcome surprise, luxuriously laid out, and with an imaginative menu of local, Greek and international dishes (heavy on grills and casseroles) which are more elegantly presented than in most places. Overall, there is a general sense of luxury in splendid isolation.

∼

NEARBY Vassilitsa ski area; hiking; riding; swimming.
LOCATION 2 km from Vassilitsa village; car parking
FOOD breakfast, lunch, dinner
PRICE €€€
ROOMS 53; 50 twin, 3 2-bedroom suites, all with en suite WC and shower; all rooms have phone, TV, balcony
FACILITIES sitting room, bar, restaurant, terrace, swimming pool, basketball, tennis
CREDIT CARDS MC, V
CHILDREN welcome
DISABLED access possible
PETS accepted
CLOSED never
PROPRIETOR Takolas SA

IOANNINA

ANO PEDINA, ZAGORIA

HOTEL AMELIKO
~ VILLAGE HOTEL ~

44008 Ano Pedina, Zagoria
TEL 0653 71501 **E-MAIL** rit-zan@otenet.gr

THIS IS A NEWLY OPENED PROPERTY on the edge of Ano Pedina village, set among old stone houses, churches, woods and pastures. The owner also operates the Kastro guesthouse, in the citadel quarter of Ioannina, and he runs a highly professional operation. From the outside, it is a dignified, grey stone building on two floors, standing a little way back from the road in a paved patio and garden filled with flowers. The open bar, reception area and restaurant have flagstone flooring, and overall the hotel manages to be both stylish and traditional, without being over-chintzy. The colour scheme is imaginative, in pretty shades of rose pink, cream and lavender, and there is plenty of polished woodwork in the bright, spacious bedrooms.

Service is better than that found in most small guesthouses in the region, with some English spoken and a reasonable level of professional promptness; you could call the Ameliko a happy combination of ancient and modern. Its surroundings are less awesomely grand than guesthouses in the higher mountain villages: it nestles in an enclosed, fertile valley ringed by wooded hills.

~

NEARBY Pindos National Park; Mt Timfi; Vikos and Aoos gorges; Drakolimni; other Zagoria villages.
LOCATION village centre
FOOD breakfast, lunch, dinner
PRICE €€
ROOMS 8 twin or double, all with shower and WC, phone
FACILITIES restaurant, terrace
CREDIT CARDS MC, V
CHILDREN welcome
DISABLED not suitable
PETS accepted by arrangement
CLOSED never
PROPRIETORS George Zannis and Miltos Rittas

IOANNINA

ANO PEDINA, ZAGORIA

TO SPITI TOU ORESTI

~ VILLAGE INN ~

44007 Ano Pedina, Zagoria
TEL and **FAX** (0653) 71202

THIS TINY INN in an unspoiled village is, to put it quite simply, the most charming place to stay in the entire Zagoria region and one of the most charming on the entire mainland.

Two cottage-style, two-storey buildings dating from the 19th century are connected by a two-tier stone paved courtyard crammed with flowers planted in red-and-blue painted olive oil cans. Inside are low coffered wood ceilings, wooden floors, and rooms painstakingly furnished with authentic antiques, such as old wooden rocking cribs, wall cupboards and chests, with shaggy *flokati* rugs or striped rag rugs on the floors.

The rooms are smallish, but this simply adds to the Spiti tou Oresti's dinky charm. Most rooms have fireplaces, and many of the beds are covered with tartan bedspreads – which should look out of place, but in fact seem just right. The service here is uniquely professional and sophisticated, and Spiti tou Oresti stands head and shoulders above its rivals in the region. Ano Pedina is a pretty and not much visited village, surrounded by wooded hills and overlooking a fertile valley, in sharp contrast to the mountain wilderness all around it.

~

NEARBY Pindos National Park; Mt Timfi; Vikos and Aoos gorges; Drakolimni; other Zagoria villages.
LOCATION village centre
FOOD breakfast, lunch, dinner
PRICE €€€
ROOMS 9 double with en suite WC and shower
FACILITIES restaurant, courtyard
CREDIT CARDS MC, V
CHILDREN welcome
DISABLED not suitable
PETS accepted by arrangement
CLOSED never
PROPRIETOR Eleni Pangratiou

IOANNINA

TO ARCHONTIKO TIS VANGELIOS
~ VILLAGE GUESTHOUSE ~

44018 Kipi, Zagoria
TEL 0653 51280

EVANGELIA'S HOUSE WOULD SUIT someone who wants to experience an authentic Zagoria home which has been little modernized (though bathrooms and plumbing are reasonably up to date). The house has a farmhouse feel, with a stone-floored entrance hall, wooden ceilings and staircase leading to the upper storey, where the rooms open off a sitting area with red-cushioned benches and picture windows. Our favourite room is the smallest, with its original wall paintings in abstract floral patterns, and a big open stone fireplace and chimney.

The house dates like many in the village, from the mid-19th century and was converted into a guesthouse in 1993 with the minimum of alterations. Evangelia is very friendly. However, guests are left to their own devices for much of the time, so this is not a place for those who expect attentive, round-the-clock service – it's more like a French self-catering *gite*, and indeed it is small enough for a family or group of friends to take over completely.

NEARBY Pindos National Park; Mt Timfi; Vikos and Aoos gorges; Drakolimni; other Zagoria villages.
LOCATION village centre
FOOD breakfast
PRICE €€
ROOMS 4 double with en suite WC and shower; all rooms have central heating
FACILITIES sitting room, courtyard
CREDIT CARDS not accepted
CHILDREN welcome
DISABLED not suitable
PETS accepted by arrangement
CLOSED never
PROPRIETOR Evangelia Derva

IOANNINA

KIPI, ZAGORIA

TO SPITI TOU ARTEMI

~ VILLAGE GUESTHOUSE ~

44018 Kipi, Zagoria
TEL 0653 51262

THE MOST REMARKABLE feature of this small village mansion is the colourful mural, said to be of the Emperor Napoleon and his mistress Josephine, which covers one wall of the pretty sitting room. Why are they there? No one seems to be sure.

This aside, the Spiti tou Artemi has simple traditional interiors with plenty of polished wood and exposed stonework, and from the roof terrace there are fine views over the valley and rolling wooded hills that surround it (pity about the ugly white plastic café chairs, though). The guesthouse is on a cobbled lane in the centre of one of the quietest and least-visited of the Zagoria villages (known for its unique arched stone bridges), and is extremely quiet, the ideal place for a low-key stay. Breakfast is served on the terrace or in the sitting room of this old mansion, originally built in 1863, but for the rest of the time you are at least partly dependent on self catering (sharing the kitchen) as Kipi has few eating or drinking places.

~

NEARBY Pindos National Park; Mt Timfi; Vikos and Aoos gorges; Drakolimni; other Zagoria villages.
LOCATION village centre
FOOD breakfast
PRICE €€
ROOMS 5 double and triple with WC and shower; all rooms have central heating, fireplace
CREDIT CARDS not accepted
CHILDREN welcome
DISABLED not suitable
PETS accepted by arrangement
CLOSED never
PROPRIETOR Mina Vlahopoulou

IOANNINA

MEGALO PAPINGO, ZAGORIA

XENODOXEIO KAITI

~ VILLAGE GUESTHOUSE ~

44016 Megalo Papingo, Zagoria
TEL 0653 41118

THIS GUESTHOUSE just outside Megalo Papingo village, below the church and beside the road to Mikro Papingo, is a sturdy, four-square new building in local style: grey stone with a heavy slate roof. It harmonizes well with the rest of the unspoiled village, and will be even more attractive when its stonework has weathered a little and when its gardens and surroundings have matured. The upstairs rooms have extraordinary views of the Astraka and Gamila crags, which tower above the village.

All the bedrooms are extremely spick and span, and are somewhat larger and lighter than those in some of the older traditional village buildings, with varnished wooden ceilings and wood floors polished to a high gloss. Owner Kaiti Panakosta is clearly house proud. This is very much a family-run business, with a family clientele too, and although the building does not have quite the weather-beaten charm of some of its competitors in the village, it makes up for it with modern comfort. There is a small bar and sitting area next to the breakfast room, and the large garden, though a bit unkempt at present, will soon be attractive.

~

NEARBY Drakolimni; Vikos gorge; other Zagoria villages.
LOCATION edge of Megalo Papingo village, on roadside
FOOD breakfast, self-catering, snacks
PRICE €€
ROOMS 6 triple with en suite WC and shower; all rooms have central heating, kitchen unit
FACILITIES sitting room, breakfast room, garden
CREDIT CARDS not accepted
CHILDREN welcome
DISABLED not suitable
PETS accepted by arrangement
CLOSED never
PROPRIETOR Kaiti Panakosta

IOANNINA

MEGALO PAPINGO, ZAGORIA

KALLIOPI

∽ VILLAGE GUESTHOUSE ∽

44016 Megalo Papingo, Zagoria
TEL 0653 41081

RATHER GRAND SCARLET-AND-BLUE-painted doors open from a stone paved lane into the large, leafy courtyard of this substantial Papingo house, with four café tables outside under a vine trellis and quite a smart-looking little restaurant and bar tucked into a corner to the right of the door. This is one of the better places to eat in Megalo Papingo (not that the village is exactly over-endowed with restaurants) and specializes in the savoury pies (filled with mutton, cheese or vegetables) that are one of the mainstays of local cooking. Also on the menu are fresh river trout, powerful local red wine from the barrel and *tsipouro* (Greek *grappa*) from the jug. Go easy on both of these: they have a high-octane effect.

Kalliopi is welcoming and family run, and the bedrooms of the carefully restored mansion house are smartly done up and decorated with traditional furniture and old tools and utensils, copper plates and earthenware pots. Surrounded by some of the most magnificent mountain scenery in Greece, it is in a very quiet location about 400 metres from the centre of Megalo Papingo.

∽

NEARBY Drakolimni; Vikos gorge; other Zagoria villages.
LOCATION edge of Megalo Papingo village
FOOD breakfast, lunch, dinner
PRICE €€€
ROOMS 7; 6 double, 1 single, all with en suite WC and shower
FACILITIES restaurant, bar, courtyard
CREDIT CARDS not accepted
CHILDREN welcome
DISABLED not suitable
PETS accepted by arrangement
CLOSED never
PROPRIETOR Kalypso Vitou

IOANNINA

MEGALO PAPINGO, ZAGORIA

PENSION KOULIS

～ VILLAGE GUESTHOUSE ～

44016 Megalo Papingo, Zagoria
TEL 0653 41138 **FAX** 0653 41115

THIS GUESTHOUSE really feels like a village inn, with its cluster of stone buildings around a cobbled courtyard under a spreading plane tree, with views of the stone houses and slate roofs of this unspoiled village. Large blue stable doors lead through a stone portico into a shady courtyard, off which are the guesthouse's own café and village shop. It is a friendly place, and has pleasant, newly furnished bedrooms with wood floors, low platform beds and a warm red and pink colour scheme.

Somebody has done a skilled job of scumble-glazing each bedroom door in a *trompe l'oeil* wood pattern, a skill which used to be common in these villages, but which is dying out. The reception area has a stone flagged floor and a dark wood ceiling, with a wooden staircase leading to the upstairs bedrooms.

Pension Koulis also offers better-than-average home cooking, with hearty and filling local dishes which are very welcome if you have just burned off several thousand calories on one of the stiff mountain walks up to the Astraka or down into the Vikos gorge.

～

NEARBY Drakolimni; Vikos gorge; other Zagoria villages.
LOCATION village centre
FOOD breakfast, dinner
PRICE ©©©©
ROOMS 6 with WC and shower
FACILITIES restaurant, courtyard
CREDIT CARDS not accepted
CHILDREN welcome
DISABLED not suitable
PETS accepted by arrangement
CLOSED never
PROPRIETOR Dimitrios Christodoulou

IOANNINA

MEGALO PAPINGO, ZAGORIA

LAKIS

∿ VILLAGE GUESTHOUSE ∿

44016 Megalo Papingo, Zagoria
TEL 0653 41087

THIS GUESTHOUSE LOOKS BUSINESSLIKE and it is one of the hubs of Megalo Papingo village life: you'll find a bit of everything here – café, restaurant, village shop and guesthouse. In short, it is what Greeks call a *magasi*, one of a vanishing breed which used to be found in almost every village but is slowly being ousted by slicker modern operations. This is a good choice if you would rather not be insulated from village life, but would like to feel part of it.

The interior is far from old fashioned, and the bedrooms which Vasileios Kotsoridis has built above his store all have modern equipment, albeit in a traditional building.

Outside is a big, leafy courtyard with a vine trellis, under the shade of a truly enormous plane tree and surrounded by cobbled lanes and other mellow old stone buildings, all overlooked by the massive, looming peaks of Astraka and Gamila (called 'the Camel' because of its humps). The courtyard makes a pleasant place to sit and watch village life go by (very slowly) and also offers off-street car parking for those who are worried about their paintwork. You should also sample, in cautious moderation, Vasileios's own wines and *tsipouro*.

∿

NEARBY Drakolimni; Vikos gorge; other Zagoria villages.
LOCATION village centre
FOOD breakfast
PRICE €€
ROOMS 8; all rooms have shower and WC
FACILITIES terrace, shop
CREDIT CARDS not accepted
CHILDREN accepted
DISABLED not suitable
PETS accepted by arrangement
CLOSED never
PROPRIETOR Vasileios Kotsoridis

IOANNINA

TO RODI
~ VILLAGE GUESTHOUSE ~

44016 Megalo Papingo, Zagoria
TEL 0653 41954

STAYING AT TO RODI will certainly keep you fit. This newish, purpose-built guesthouse in the traditional style is the highest building in the village, and it's a steep climb up a cobbled lane from the centre. Nevertheless, this altitude guarantees you the best view in town of the surrounding mountains and gorges, which is saying something. The Zagoria villages specialize in million-dollar views at a bargain price, and To Rodi is no exception.

To Rodi is surrounded by a grassy garden with flowers, shrubs and nut trees. The lower floor is arcaded with a front door opening into a ground-floor sitting room where an open fire is lit in the cooler months. (High above sea level, this part of Greece gets snow and freezing weather in winter, and the fire is just as welcome on spring and autumn evenings when there is a nip in the air.) Megalo Papingo hardly suffers from hubbub at any time, but To Rodi is almost deafeningly quiet. You could easily spend a week (or more) unwinding here, so long as you bring plenty of books to read. None of the Papingo guesthouses have pools, but there is a natural swimming pool, formed by damming the local stream, about ten minutes' walk from the village.

~

NEARBY Drakolimni; Vikos gorge; other Zagoria villages.
LOCATION above centre of Megalo Papingo village
FOOD breakfast
PRICE €€
ROOMS 6 twin, 2 with extra bed, all with shower and WC
FACILITIES sitting room, garden
CREDIT CARDS not accepted
CHILDREN welcome
DISABLED not suitable
PETS by arrangement
CLOSED never
PROPRIETOR Dimitrios Tzomakas

IOANNINA

MEGALO PAPINGO, ZAGORIA

TA SPITIA TOU SAXONI

~ VILLAGE GUESTHOUSE ~

44016 Megalo Papingo, Zagoria
TEL 0653 41615

WITH THEIR STURDY STONE WALLS, iron-barred windows, wooden outside staircases and leafy vines giving shade to doors and windows, the Saxoni Houses are superb examples of the lovely traditional architecture of the Zagoria villages.

Three separate buildings, dating from 1750, 1840 and 1900, have been restored by their owner, Nikos Saxonis, and must be among the very best places to stay in the beautiful, unspoiled traditional village of Megalo Papingo. While the exterior is historically correct, the interior combines modern comforts with traditional furnishings, exposed stonework and polished wood floors and stairs.

The houses stand around a cool, shady courtyard which is a great place to sit in summer (when breakfast and snacks are served outdoors); while in cooler seasons the lounge has a welcoming open fireplace. There is no full-service restaurant, but coffee, drinks (including local wines and regional *tsipouro*) and snacks are served in the breakfast room or the courtyard all day. The Saxoni Houses have been open only since 1990, but have built up a strong international following, and it is essential to book early if you plan to visit during the busy Greek Easter and in July and August.

~

NEARBY Vikos Gorge; Aoos National Park; Mt Timfi.
LOCATION 53 km N of Ioannina
FOOD breakfast, snacks
PRICE €€
ROOMS 8 twin with bath, 5 with fireplaces
FACILITIES breakfast room, garden courtyard
CREDIT CARDS not accepted
CHILDREN welcome
DISABLED access difficult
PETS accepted **CLOSED** never
PROPRIETOR Nikos Saxonis

IOANNINA

MONODENDRI, ZAGORIA

ARCHONTIKO ZARKADA
∼ VILLAGE GUESTHOUSE ∼

44007 Monodendri, Zagoria
TEL 0653 71305 **FAX** 0653 71405

STANDING JUST ABOVE the road in one of the Zagoria region's more visited villages (close to the path into the splendid Vikos gorge) the Zarkada is a modern building in local materials, incorporating traditional design features in what seems a rather uneasy compromise: perhaps it will mellow with time. The local stone, which splits naturally into handy, square-edged blocks, is a boon to masons, but it does give newer buildings such as the Zarkada an initially harsh appearance, which takes some years to soften.

Appearances aside, the Zarkada is a comfortable small inn with two leafy courtyards and is located in what (by Zagoria standards) is quite a lively village, with a choice of eating places (including the grill restaurant next door). There are fine views, and as a base for a hike into the Vikos gorge or for exploring Zagoria by car this competently run modern guesthouse has much to recommend it. It is small enough to feel intimate and cosy, and the rooms are comfortable and modern with new furniture and a neutral colour scheme. An ideal place for guests who want a slightly higher level of service than most of the region's smaller, family-run inns can offer, and who do not want to be bothered with looking for themselves.

∼

NEARBY Pindos National Park; Mt Timfi; Vikos and Aoos gorges; Drakolimni; other Zagoria villages.
LOCATION village centre
FOOD breakfast
PRICE ⓔⓔⓔ
ROOMS 6 double and twin with en suite WC and shower
FACILITIES 2 sitting rooms, courtyard
CREDIT CARDS MC, V
CHILDREN welcome
DISABLED not suitable
PETS accepted
CLOSED never
PROPRIETOR Vasilios Zarkadas

IOANNINA

MONODENDRI, ZAGORIA

XENONAS VIKOS

~ VILLAGE GUESTHOUSE ~

44007 Monodendri, Zagoria
TEL 0653 71370

JUST OFF THE lower square of Monodendri village (one square is on the main road, the other under plane trees below the main road, reached by steep cobbled paths), the Vikos is certainly the most convenient jumping-off point for a hike into the 900-m deep Vikos gorge, which is only 400 m from the front door. The two-storey building is stone-built with the usual slate roof and pine shutters, and a pleasant walled courtyard.

The views are not much, but the place is a comfortable compromise between inn and hostel, serving breakfast in the courtyard or indoors in cooler weather, and offers guests the use of shared kitchen facilities.

The owner of the guesthouse, Mr Paterakis, is also proprietor of one of two *tavernas* on the lower square, and is full of useful information about the village and the region. The guesthouse has a comfortable sitting room, where you can rest up after hiking the gorge. One of the better bases for exploring the Zagoria villages and the pocket wilderness of the Pindos National Park region.

~

NEARBY Pindos National Park; Mt Timfi; Vikos and Aoos gorges; Drakolimni; other Zagoria villages.
LOCATION village centre
FOOD breakfast, self-catering
PRICE €€
ROOMS 7 double and triple with en suite WC and shower; all rooms have phone
FACILITIES kitchen, courtyard
CREDIT CARDS MC, V
CHILDREN accepted
DISABLED not suitable
PETS accepted by arrangement
CLOSED Jan-Feb
PROPRIETOR Emmanoulis Paterakis

IOANNINA

TSEPELOVO, ZAGORIA

TO ARCHONTIKO
∼ TRADITIONAL GUESTHOUSE ∼

44010 Tsepelovo, Zagoria
TEL 0653 81216

T HE ARCHONTIKO STANDS out in a village of almost monochrome old stone cottages and mansions, with its bright blue and yellow wooden upper floor and arched windows perched above the three larger arches of its ground floor, which open onto a pleasant paved patio full of roses and chrysanthemums. Breakfast tables stand in the shade beneath these arches.

On a quiet cobbled lane in one of the Zagoria region's most beautiful mountain villages, this is an outstanding spot for an extremely relaxing stay, though there are also opportunities for strenuous mountain and gorge walking in one of Greece's highest mountain ranges and in the deepest canyon in Europe. Built in 1787, the house was restored and opened as an inn in 1992, and was one of the first traditional guesthouses in a village where there are now two or three.

It is still definitely one of the pleasantest, with a first-floor dining room where you can eat local dishes. It is not, however, a full-service hotel and you must phone in advance to make sure someone is on hand to let you in, as the reception is not continuously staffed.

∼

NEARBY Mt Timfi; Vikos gorge; Drakolimni.
LOCATION centre of village
FOOD breakfast
PRICE €€
ROOMS 6; 5 double, 1 triple, 3 with en suite WC and shower
FACILITIES breakfast room, courtyard
CREDIT CARDS not accepted
CHILDREN welcome
DISABLED not suitable
PETS accepted by arrangement
CLOSED never
PROPRIETOR Mairi Tsavalias

IOANNINA

TSEPELOVO, ZAGORIA

FANIS'S GUESTHOUSE

~ VILLAGE GUESTHOUSE ~

44010 Tsepelovo, Zagoria
TEL 0653 81271

FANIS'S GUESTHOUSE is in the upper part of Tsepelovo village and the views of the massive mountains which surround it are stupendous, especially from the two front-upper bedrooms.

The owners, Fanis Tzavalias and his family, are very friendly and have been running this sturdy, 150-year-old stone building with its blue woodwork (rather faded last time we visited) as an inn since the mid-1980s. This is very much a family home, with Fanis and his father both doing the cooking (on request rather than from a menu) and serving local dishes accompanied by their own wine, which must be tried, though it may not find favour with more sophisticated palates.

Fanis also guides visitors on mountain walks and treks of all durations among the totally unspoiled villages and breathtaking scenery of the Zagoria region. He is also expanding his operation by building a brand new extension to the inn, in local stone, just opposite, and tells us that he hopes this will be completed in time for the summer 2002 season, adding eight new rooms.

~

NEARBY Mt Timfi; Vikos and Aoos gorges; Drakolimni; other Zagoria villages
LOCATION above main square of Tsepelovo village.
FOOD breakfast
PRICE ⓔⓔ
ROOMS 8; 5 twin, 3 family, all with en suite WC and shower; 8 rooms to be added by 2002/3
FACILITIES sitting room
CREDIT CARDS not accepted
CHILDREN welcome
DISABLED not suitable
PETS accepted
CLOSED never
PROPRIETOR Fanis Tzavalias

IOANNINA

TSEPELOVO, ZAGORIA

HAYATI HOTEL

~ VILLAGE HOTEL ~

44010 Tsepelovo, Zagoria
TEL and **FAX** 0653 81301

A NEW AND PROFESSIONAL ADDITION to Tsepelovo's range of accommodation, the Hayati is a mellow stone building with wooden balconies on the upper floors, stone roof and deep eaves – in other words, it has been built entirely in the style of the village and from local materials. Stone steps lead to a covered porch, and within is a cosy reception, bar and sitting room area, eclectically decorated – heavily embroidered traditional costumes in frames hang on the walls next to old maps of the area, and a belt of .50 calibre machine gun bullets (no longer live, we trust) hangs behind the reception desk, while old earthenware jars sit on shelves and in niches.

The rooms are large, bright studios, each with a two-ring cooker and sink unit, TV and phone, and are simply and cleanly furnished with wooden beds and bright blankets. Some rooms have balconies with smashing panoramic views, inspiring to wake up to.

Just outside the front door is a small patio terrace with three café tables, a charming place in which to have breakfast, morning coffee or evening drinks. The Hayati is family run, and very friendly, with more facilities than many Zagoria guesthouses.

~

NEARBY Pindos National Park; Mt Timfi; Vikos and Aoos gorges; Drakolimni; other Zagoria villages.
LOCATION village centre
FOOD breakfast
PRICE €€€
ROOMS 8 studios with en suite WC and shower; all studios have phone, TV, central heating, kitchenette
FACILITIES sitting room, bar, terrace
CREDIT CARDS not accepted
CHILDREN welcome
DISABLED not suitable
PETS accepted by arrangement
CLOSED never
PROPRIETOR Kostas Glinavos

IOANNINA

I MIKRI ARKTOS

~ VILLAGE INN ~

44010 Tsepelovo, Zagoria
TEL 0653 81128

THIS TINY GUESTHOUSE, above the village *taverna* and overlooking a wide, stone-flagged square shaded by an enormous plane tree and full of café tables where the locals gather to sit and play backgammon, is brand new and utterly delightful. Each of its three rooms is large, with double or twin beds, and each is decorated thematically, with the bright-coloured, wooden ceilings setting the tone for bedspreads, soft furnishings and other touches.

One room has an emerald green ceiling, one is royal blue, and the third is deep red. Such decoration is traditional in the wealthier family homes of the Zagoria villages, a region with a fascinating history. Less traditional, perhaps, are the self-catering kitchen units in each room, allowing you to prepare coffee, tea or breakfast in your own time. The Mikri Arktos – the name means 'The Little Bear' – feels very much like a comfortable inn, though the substantial and busy *taverna* downstairs, which has high, arched windows and blue and white woodwork, is actually separately owned and run. At night, the only sound you will hear is the sighing of the wind in the branches outside your bedroom window.

~

NEARBY Pindos National Park; Mt Timfi; Vikos and Aoos gorges; Drakolimni; other Zagoria villages.
LOCATION village centre
FOOD breakfast
PRICE €€
ROOMS 3 with WC and shower
FACILITIES *taverna* (separate management)
CREDIT CARDS not accepted
CHILDREN welcome
DISABLED not suitable
PETS accepted by arrangement
CLOSED never
PROPRIETOR Kitas G. Thomas

IOANNINA

VITSA, ZAGORIA

ARCHONTIKO DANOU

~ VILLAGE GUESTHOUSE ~

44007 Vitsa, Zagoria
TEL 0653 71371

THIS IS ONE of the oldest buildings in the region, dating from the 17th century and it stands on a cobbled pathway high above the village, seeming to grow out of the rock on which it is built, and draped in ivy and creepers. The tall, mellow old building has a pleasingly ramshackle air, but which some may find a little off-putting. It is impeccably authentic inside, with old wooden furniture, red and black rugs and cushions, and painted and varnished woodwork; you feel that you have stepped into a slice of local history.

Breakfast is the only meal served, but there is a *taverna* just a couple of minutes' walk away, on the main road through the village. The Danou produces its own wine, cheese and *tsipouro* (the *grappa* of Greece) all of which can be bought to take away.

Finally, there are grand views from the balcony and from the upper windows of the guesthouse over the grey stone walls and roofs of Vikos village. This is arguably the most historically authentic of all the Zagoria mansions, and appeals to people who really appreciate a historical experience.

~

NEARBY Pindos National Park; Mt Timfi; Vikos and Aoos gorges; Drakolimni; other Zagoria villages.
LOCATION above village centre
FOOD breakfast
PRICE ©©
ROOMS 5 triple with en suite WC and shower
FACILITIES sitting room
CREDIT CARDS not accepted
CHILDREN accepted
DISABLED not suitable
PETS accepted
CLOSED never
PROPRIETOR Alexandros Vatavalis

IOANNINA

KASTRO, IOANNINA

XENODOXEIO FILYRA

~ TOWN HOTEL ~

Andronikos Palaiogou 18, 45221 Kastro, Ioannina
TEL 0651 83560/093 2257290

THIS BRAND NEW SMALL HOTEL is one of several places to stay within the ancient stone walls of Ioannina's medieval castle. It is tiny, attractively painted pink and blue, and stands in a very narrow street. There is very little accommodation in the quiet old quarter of Ioannina, within the ramparts and close to the lake, and this little hotel would be an excellent base for leisurely exploration of Ioannina and the region. Lake-front restaurants and boats to the lake island are within two minutes' walk, as is the Byzantine Museum. Worth mentioning, too, is the outstandingly pretty Café Filistron, next door, brightly painted in crimson and turquoise inside and serving drinks, coffee, traditional sweets and snacks.

~

NEARBY Byzantine museum; lake island; medieval fortress; mosques.
LOCATION town centre, within walled old quarter of Ioannina
FOOD breakfast, self-catering
PRICE €€€
ROOMS 5 self-contained studio apartments with WC and shower, kitchen unit
FACILITIES courtyard
CREDIT CARDS MC, V
CHILDREN accepted
DISABLED not suitable
PETS accepted by arrangement
CLOSED never
PROPRIETOR Hotel Filyra

IOANNINA

KASTRO, IOANNINA

HOTEL KASTRO

~ TOWN HOTEL ~

Andronikos Palaiogou 57, 45221 Kastro, Ioannina
TEL 0651 83560/093 2257290

THIS ATTRACTIVELY DECORATED and restored hotel opposite the Byzantine Museum, within the walls of Ioannina's old citadel, is the best address in the historic capital of the Epirus region. The Kastro is in an old mansion house, on one corner of a quiet square, with a sunny, private courtyard; flowering shrubs and shady trees adorn the front door area.

The ground floor has a cool, open-plan bar, reception and breakfast area. A stone staircase leads up to bedrooms which open off a large lobby, smartly painted in red and gold crackle-glaze and cream, with panelled wooden walls, and tapestry covered seating. The bedrooms are essentially modern, but with antique brass beds complementing up-to-date equipment. Side tables are marble topped, and the en suite bathrooms are mostly marble too. The owners, George Zannis and Miltos Rittas, who also own the Hotel Ameliko in Ano Pedina, speak good English and run a friendly and professional operation. Service is personal and friendly, and the atmosphere and all the attractions of this historic town, including a fascinating Byzantine museum housed in an Ottoman mosque, are on your doorstep

~

NEARBY Lake Pamvotis and island; citadel; Byzantine museum.
LOCATION town centre, within old quarter
FOOD breakfast
PRICE €€€
ROOMS 7 double and triple with WC and shower; all rooms have phone, TV
FACILITIES breakfast room, bar, courtyard
CREDIT CARDS MC, V
CHILDREN accepted
DISABLED not suitable
PETS accepted by arrangement
CLOSED never
PROPRIETORS George Zannis and Miltos Rittas

IOANNINA

KAMARES

~ TRADITIONAL GUESTHOUSE ~

Zalokosta 74, 45221 Ioannina
TEL 0651 79348 **Fax** 0651 40286
website http://www.epcon.gr/kamares/

KAMARES IS A newly restored, 116-year-old mansion in a formerly dilapi-dated district, near the lake and the Turkish-Byzantine castle, which is being cheerfully restored, with many of its traditional buildings becoming trendy restaurants.

It is built around an old stone courtyard (one room, 112, is at the back of this, the others in the main house). The reception opens on to a vault-ed, cellar-like bar with inlaid wooden benches and vivid textiles, and has something of the atmosphere of a village inn.

Upstairs, the rooms on the first floor are comfortable and newly deco-rated, but bland, with whitewashed walls and wood ceilings. Ask instead for a room on the top floor, where the attic rooms with sloping loft ceilings have much more character. The staff are friendly (though they speak only fragmentary English) and the place is kept spotless.

Kamares can be hard to find and the street numbers are misleading: Zalokosta Street extends beyond its apparent northern end and numbers 72 and 74 do not appear at first sight to follow on from number 70. You may need to call the hotel for directions.

~

NEARBY Kastro; Byzantine museum; Lake Pamvotis.
LOCATION close to town centre and historic citadel
FOOD breakfast
PRICE €€€
ROOMS 8 double and 1 suite, all with en suite WC and shower; all rooms have phone, TV, air conditioning, fan, minibar
FACILITIES sitting room, bar
CREDIT CARDS not accepted
CHILDREN accepted
DISABLED not suitable
PETS not accepted
CLOSED never
PROPRIETORS Kamares

METSOVO

HOTEL FLOKAS
~ VILLAGE HOTEL ~

44200 Metsovo
TEL and FAX 0656 41309

THE FLOKAS IS A FAIRLY MODERN BUILDING, but true to the traditional style of the Metsovo region both inside and out. Built of local stone, it has a small lobby and breakfast room over which the father of the family presides most of the time, and the interior is almost entirely in polished pine, with bits and bobs of ornate carpentry, such as wall friezes and decorative ceiling roses, in the hall and in the rooms. On the first floor is a tiny stone fountain which emits the soothing sound of trickling water.

The rooms are on the small side, but very snug, with enclosed balconies over the street, lovely bird's eye views over the stone roofs and streets of this unspoiled village, and pine walls and ceilings. Bathrooms are modern, and we were impressed with the limitless hot water and high-powered shower. The TV, mounted on an ugly bracket high up on the wall, is rather incongruous in these otherwise very traditional rooms. The TV in the downstairs lobby has Sky TV, handy for those Anglophones who yearn to catch up with international news or sports results. The Flokas is a friendly, family-run sort of place, and we recommend it.

~

NEARBY Metsova; Valia Kalda National Park; Tositsa Museum.
LOCATION village centre
FOOD breakfast
PRICE €€
ROOMS 10 double, all with en suite shower and WC, enclosed balcony
FACILITIES sitting room
CREDIT CARDS not accepted
CHILDREN welcome
DISABLED not suitable
PETS not accepted
CLOSED never
PROPRIETOR Mihali Mertzanis

TRIKALA

ELATI

TO LIGERI

∼ VILLAGE HOTEL ∼

42032 Elati, Trikala
Tel and **Fax** 0434 71454
E-**mail** info@ligerihotel.gr

WITH ITS PALE STONE WALLS, white painted window surrounds and white-washed upper storey with wooden balconies, this small guesthouse in a pretty mountain village below pine-forested crags is the most charming place to stay at in Elati. The surroundings are grand, and there are some great walks in the woods and hills around Elati. Outside the front door of the hotel, white canvas director's chairs cluster around café tables on a stone patio, surrounded by pots of red and purple flowers on window sills and walls. Inside, the Ligeri has very much the atmosphere of a village inn, with tiled floors, wooden benches and couches in front of a big stone fireplace, and copper dishes decorating the stone walls. Because the hotel is right beside the main road which passes through the village there could be some traffic noise during the day, but this is not a busy highway and there is very little traffic at night. The rooms are neutrally decorated, with striped woollen bed-covers, and each has a balcony or, on the ground floor, its own little patio among grass and shrubs. All things considered, To Ligeri would be a fine place to stay overnight on a touring holiday, or for a few nights to explore the surrounding scenery on foot. There are numerous pleasant restaurants in the village.

∼

NEARBY Ligeri village; mountain walks; Meteora monasteries.
LOCATION centre of village, on main street
FOOD breakfast
PRICE €€
ROOMS 10 with en suite WC and shower; all rooms have balcony or terrace
FACILITIES sitting room, bar
CREDIT CARDS not accepted
CHILDREN welcome
DISABLED not suitable
PETS accepted by arrangement
CLOSED never
PROPRIETORS Xenodoxrion Ligeri SA

TRIKALA

PERTOULI

ARCHONTIKO DIVANI
∼ VILLAGE HOTEL ∼

Pertouli, Trikala
TEL and FAX 0434 91252

THIS IS A BRAND NEW HOTEL, albeit one constructed in immaculate local style, built of dove-grey limestone with a slate roof, tall chimneys and a varnished wooden balcony jutting from the upper storey.

The young owner, Dimitris Divanis, is enthusiastic, friendly and full of advice about things to do and places to see in this delightfully undiscovered mountain region. It will be an even better place to stay when its surroundings have matured a little (and when the building work opposite has been completed).

Pine woods and bare mountains make for grand views, and logs piled beneath the overhanging balconies indicate that blazing log fires will be lit on cool autumn and winter evenings.

Inside, there are coffered wooden ceilings, tiled floors, and walls hung with family antiques – chased silver flintlock pistols, heavily embroidered wedding costumes, and beautiful silver jewellery. The rooms are unfussy, well thought-out, and comfortable for winter or summer, with plenty of daylight. Most, but not all, have fine views (some overlook the building site mentioned above).

∼

NEARBY Pertouli; Meteora monasteries.
LOCATION 500 m from Pertouli village centre
FOOD breakfast, lunch, dinner
PRICE €€€
ROOMS 10 double or twin, all with en suite shower and WC, TV, phone
FACILITIES sitting room, restaurant
CREDIT CARDS MC, V
CHILDREN welcome
DISABLED not suitable
PETS accepted by arrangement
CLOSED never
PROPRIETOR Dimitris Divanis

TRIKALA

PERTOULI

ARCHONTIKO HADZIGAKI

~ COUNTRY HOUSE HOTEL ~

Pertouli, Trikala
TEL 0434 91146 FAX 0434 91166

THIS DIGNIFIED MANSION HOUSE, built of solid grey stone with a slate roof, is an outstanding discovery, located in a very quiet village among hills and pine woods. The main house stands among terraces and green clover lawns, while a separate wing contains more rooms and the reception area. Rooms and separate buildings, including the hotel's own small *taverna*, are linked by paved, wheelchair-friendly ramps and paths.

Within, rooms feel like independent cottages, with sloping wooden ceilings, wooden beds and large, cosy duvets and luxurious bathrooms with huge tubs. Clearly, this hotel is geared up for winter as well as summer visitors. There are wooden cupboards and antique wood chests and benches in the rooms and along the corridors. The grounds are shaded by tall cedars and ash trees, and the hotel even has its own small chapel for weddings and other family ceremonies. The large open-air pool has great views. All in all, a superb mountain retreat, almost unique in Greece, and ideal for a short or longer stay, with several small *tavernas* in the village should you wish a wider choice of eating places.

~

NEARBY Pertouli; Meteora monasteries.
LOCATION edge of Pertouli village, set back from road; car parking
FOOD breakfast, lunch, dinner
PRICE ©©©©
ROOMS 20 single, double, triple and suites
FACILITIES restaurant, garden, swimming pool
CREDIT CARDS MC, V
CHILDREN welcome
DISABLED access possible
PETS accepted
CLOSED never
PROPRIETOR Dimitrios Hadzigakis

TRIKALA

KYNIGI

~ COUNTRY GUESTHOUSE ~

Vitoumas, Kaloneri, Trikala
TEL 0431 86660

ORIGINALLY A SHOOTING LODGE, the Kynigi still attracts Greek and Italian sportsmen in season (late September to February). The L-shaped, ranch-style building has a large garden, and its ten adjoining rooms are prettily painted in blue and yellow, with a red tiled roof.

There is a large, open-air barbecue restaurant with benches and trestle tables in the garden, and the reception area is one large open-plan space with restaurant tables and a fireplace. Service is lackadaisical except at mealtimes, and there is little to do except to enjoy the pastoral surroundings: it sits among woods and fields and there's a small stream at the foot of the garden. Still, this is the only place of character in the Kalambaka area, where most accommodation is in bland touring hotels or in campsites, and the Kyniyi is a pleasant enough stopover when visiting the remarkable rock formations and monasteries of the Meteora.

One caution: the hotel is not easy to find. Follow the signs to Vitoumas monastery (M. Vitoumas), not to Vitoulas village.

~

NEARBY Meteora monasteries.
LOCATION 7 km SW of Kalambaka, 10 km from Meteora; car parking
FOOD breakfast, lunch, dinner
PRICE €€€
ROOMS 0 double with en suite WC and shower; all rooms have fireplace
FACILITIES restaurant, garden
CREDIT CARDS not accepted
CHILDREN accepted
DISABLED access possible
PETS accepted
CLOSED never
PROPRIETOR Christina Legka

KARDITSA

ANATOLI

~ COUNTRY HOTEL ~

Neohori, Karditsa
TEL 0441 93063 **FAX** 0441 93190

THIS UNPRETENTIOUS SMALL hotel has a grand view of Lake Plastiras and is set on a steep slope, below a quiet country road and among green fields and woodland, in a region of central Greece so far almost completely undiscovered by foreigners.

Nearby are the picturesque, hidden villages of the Agrapha mountains, and there is fishing and a choice of water sports on the man-made lake, created by damming one of Greece's major rivers in the 1950s.

The Anatoli has a large all-in-one bar, reception and lobby area (grander than you would expect from its simple, pine and whitewashed plaster exterior), modern in design, with soft sofas and armchairs, and the restaurant serves good local food, with emphasis on stews, casseroles and some game dishes in season. Outside is a large balcony, with potted geraniums and sweeping views.

The Anatoli's bedrooms are simply and comfortably furnished, nothing to get excited about; all have private balconies with lake views. This is not, perhaps, a hotel for a long stay, but is certainly a comfortable, friendly place to spend a night or two while exploring this very different, little known and completely unspoiled region of mainland Greece.

~

NEARBY Lake Plastiras.
LOCATION outskirts of Neohori village, W shore of Lake Plastiras; car parking
FOOD breakfast, lunch, dinner
PRICE ©©©
ROOMS 27 double with en suite WC and shower; all rooms have phone, central heating
FACILITIES bar, restaurant
CREDIT CARDS not accepted
CHILDREN accepted
DISABLED not suitablele **PETS** accepted
CLOSED never
PROPRIETORS Limnis Nik. Plastira AE

KARDITSA

NEOHORI

NAIADES

~ COUNTRY HOTEL ~

Neohori, Karditsa
TEL 0441 93333 **FAX** 0441 93173

THIS COUNTRY CLUB-STYLE HOTEL in the middle of forested countryside, on the shore of a long, mirror-calm man-made lake, is a remarkable find. The Naiades is a new hotel, and has so far been discovered only by a Greek clientele . Ideal for active families, it has a large pool (with views from its terrace across the lake shore, which is used as an airstrip by microlight pilots). Basketball and tennis courts complete the array of activities on hand. The stone buildings use local materials and are in local style, blending in well with their surroundings.

Inside, the lobby area is separated from the main restaurant by arched, indoor windows and has a clubby, exclusive feel, with big leather armchairs and sofas and an expensive jeweller's shop. Extending around the outside of the restaurant is a balcony, for outdoor dining in summer, though this hotel appears equally popular with Greek visitors in winter.

The hotel is built on a slope, so the pool and its terrace are immediately below the restaurant. Rooms are expansive and modern, with dark wood coffee tables and chequered quilted bedspreads, and are decorated in neutral colours.

~

NEARBY Lake Plastiras.
LOCATION below Neohori village, on W shore of Lake Plastiras
FOOD breakfast, lunch, dinner
PRICE €€€€
ROOMS 50 double and triple, all with en suite shower and WC, balcony or terrace, phone, TV, minibar
FACILITIES sitting room, bar, restaurant, terrace, swimming pool, basketball, tennis
CREDIT CARDS MC, V
CHILDREN welcome
DISABLED access possible
PETS accepted
CLOSED never
PROPRIETORS Nevropolis AE

MAGNESIA

AGIOS GEORGIOS, PILION

ARCHONTIKO DERELI

~ TRADITIONAL INN ~

38500 Agios Georgios, Pilion
TEL 0428 98221 **FAX** 0428 93163

AGIOS GEORGIOS, on the west slope of the Pilion peninsula and around 18 km from Volos, is a working village (the wine barrels and olive oil jars stacked around its old stone homes are obvious clues) and is much less chi-chi than many. Only a couple of its traditional mansions have been done up, and the Dereli is one of the friendliest places to stay in the region.

You enter from a narrow lane, just below a substantial village church, into a small stone courtyard under the shade of kiwi fruit vines. Inside are five rooms, grouped around one of the shared sitting areas so typical of these old houses, with many windows to let in the light, panelled benches built against the walls and covered with stripy red and yellow wool cushions, and shaggy, brightly coloured *flokati* wool rugs. Coloured glass skylights above the windows let in more light and add still more colour.

The breakfast room, in a separate small building in the courtyard, is a real farmhouse kitchen, with chequered red and white table cloths, huge wooden beams, and farm implements and old shotguns hanging on the walls. If you are looking for a typical, authentic Pilion family home, this is it.

~

NEARBY beach at Kala Nera; Volos; Milies; Vizitsa; Pilion railway.
LOCATION in village centre beside church; car parking
FOOD breakfast; lunch and dinner on request
PRICE €€€
ROOMS 5 with shared WC and bath
FACILITIES breakfast room, courtyard
CREDIT CARDS not accepted
CHILDREN welcome
DISABLED not suitable
PETS not accepted
CLOSED never
PROPRIETOR M. Dereli

MAGNESIA

AGIOS GEORGIOS, PILION

ARCHONTIKO TZORTZI

~ TRADITIONAL INN ~

38500 Agios Georgios, Pilion
TEL 0428 94252 **FAX** 0428 94293

BUILT IN 1861, this listed historic building is strikingly different from most of its Pilion rivals. Its pale-pink stucco front, white plaster detailing and tall blue-painted shutters owe more to neoclassical architecture than to Pilion tradition.

The house is built on two storeys, with a large, light breakfast room and sitting room on the ground floor, and bedrooms upstairs. Rooms are bright and airy and attractively furnished, offering a mixture of modern comfort and traditional style. The courtyard is a very agreeable place to sit, read, snooze or drink coffee or an evening *ouzo*.

The Archontiko Tzortzi does not have the sweeping views of some of its rivals, but is pleasantly quiet and well off the beaten track. The village *plateia*, with a choice of places to sit, eat, drink and play backgammon, is only 20 m away. The only snag is the distance from the sea; the nearest place to swim is a good 25 minutes' drive on some very demanding roads. If the beach isn't a major holiday priority, though, this is an attractive place to stay – more like your own private villa than a hotel.

~

NEARBY Kala Nera beach; Milies; Vizitsa; Pilion railway.
LOCATION Agios Georgios village centre, 100 m above main road (steep path)
FOOD breakfast
PRICE €€€
ROOMS 7 twin, all en suite with WC
FACILITIES garden
CREDIT CARDS DC, MC, V
CHILDREN welcome
DISABLED not suitable
PETS not accepted
CLOSED never
PROPRIETOR Evanthia Patsiada

MAGNESIA

AGIOS IOANNIS, PILION

HOTEL ALOE
~ BEACH HOTEL ~

37012 Agios Ioannis, Pilion
TEL 0426 31240 **FAX** 0426 31341 **E-MAIL** htl-aloe@otenet.gr

SET BACK ABOUT 50 M from the quiet waterfront of a delightful, unspoiled little resort with a fine white sand and pebble beach, the Hotel Aloe is an ideal compromise place to stay for anyone who wants to be near the natural beauty of the Pilion countryside but for whom the beach is important too.

The Aloe is larger than most of the hotels we have included, but makes it into this guide on the strength of its location and an architectural style which is influenced by the local vernacular. With its spacious green lawns under tall trees, one observer found the Aloe oddly reminiscent of a British colonial hotel or game lodge in Africa, while others have said it reminds them of one of Greece's historic monasteries. There is nothing monastic about the facilities, however. Public areas are open-plan and plain, with breakfast tables indoors or under the arches of the arcade that runs along the front of the building. All rooms have balconies, but specify a room at the front, with a sea view.

There is no pool, but with an excellent beach so close, who needs one? Although an esplanade runs between the beach and the hotel it carries very little traffic.

~

NEARBY beach; Pilion villages.
LOCATION S end of Agios Ioannis village; car parking
FOOD breakfast, snacks
PRICE €€€
ROOMS 45 twin with en suite WC and shower; all rooms have phone
FACILITIES breakfast room, lift, garden
CREDIT CARDS MC, V
CHILDREN welcome
DISABLED access possible
PETS not accepted
CLOSED never
PROPRIETOR Panagiotis Mitsiou

MAGNESIA

DAMOUCHARI, PILION

HOTEL DAMOUCHARI

~ BEACH HOTEL ~

Damouchari, Pilion
TEL and **FAX** 0426 49840/41

SET CLOSE TO A PRISTINE white pebble beach in a tiny fishing hamlet (little more than a couple of houses and two or three *tavernas* by a natural harbour), the delightful, eclectically stylish Hotel Damouchari is one of the most charming places to stay in all of Greece.

The hotel stands on the family's land, and owners Apostolis and Elli have turned an unpromising patch of thorn-covered wilderness into a veritable Eden of green lawns, shade trees and flowering shrubs, among which stand two-storey cottages built in the traditional Pilion style, with overhanging wooden balconies. Newly built, the hotel deserves praise for sensitive design and landscaping, and in no way mars the gorgeous Pilion landscape of bright blue sea, white cliffs and thick green forest.

Each room is individually and colourfully decorated, with pebble mosaics in the shower, and the friendly bar and lobby/reception area are eclectically decorated with antiques and curios discovered by Apostolos in local villages. The hotel is used by several European holiday companies which block-book rooms, so it is essential to make your reservation well in advance – the place is often full.

~

NEARBY Mt Pilion; Volos archaeological site; Pilion narrow-gauge railway.
LOCATION 1 minute walk from the sea
FOOD breakfast
PRICE ⓔⓔⓔ
ROOMS 8 double with WC and shower, 8 apartments with kitchenette
FACILITIES garden, bar, snack restaurant
CREDIT CARDS MC, V
CHILDREN welcome
DISABLED not suitable
PETS accepted
CLOSED Oct-Apr
PROPRIETORS Apostolos and Eleftheria Bainopoulou

MAGNESIA

KOROPI, PILION

SAILY BEACH HOTEL
~ SEASIDE HOTEL ~

37010 Koropi, Pilion
TEL 0423 22044 **FAX** 0428 23075 **E-MAIL** saily@argo.net.gr

THE SAILY BEACH (WE THINK they mean 'Shelly Beach') is a simple small hotel, designed with a nod to Pilion architectural style and standing just off the not very busy main road among olive groves and fields full of flowers, sheep and goats. Beyond doubt, it's one of the best spots in Pilion for a family holiday. The hotel also has its own large new pool and outdoor Jacuzzi. Water flows from the Jacuzzi into the main pool, making a soothing background sound. Akti Koropi, an uncrowded, clean Blue Flag beach, is just a few metres away and has loungers, sun umbrellas and a café. The pebbly beach stretches for miles.

The Saily Beach has a large, open-plan reception area and breakfast room, opening on to a sunny terrace shaded by a vine arbour from which lush bunches of grapes dangle in season. Half the rooms are in a newly-built wing (which contains the reception and breakfast room) and are spacious and well designed with polished wood floors, double beds with patch-work quilts, and built-in wardrobes. The older rooms, in the original hotel, were built some 25 years ago and are the smallest. On our last inspection they were showing their age, but were being refurbished.

~

NEARBY Akti Koropi beach; Milies; Vizitsa; Volos.
LOCATION Koropi village, 100 m from sea on Gulf of Volos
FOOD breakfast, lunch, dinner
PRICE €€
ROOMS 28 twin
FACILITIES restaurant, bar, breakfast room, café terrace, swimming pool
CREDIT CARDS MC, V
CHILDREN welcome
DISABLED suitable
PETS not accepted
CLOSED never
PROPRIETOR Dimitra Agrigianni

MAGNESIA

MAKRINITSA, PILION

XENONAS KARAMARLI

∽ TRADITIONAL MANSION ∽

37011 Makrinitsa, Pilion
TEL 0428 99570 **FAX** 0428 99779

T HE TRADITIONAL MANSION houses of the Pilion apple-growing villages are among the most beautiful in Greece, with extensive use of hardwoods and decorative coloured glass windows, slate roofs and overhanging upper storeys. Many have now been converted to guesthouses, and this lovingly restored 18thC family home is a particularly fine example in one of the prettiest and certainly the easiest to get to of the Pilion villages.

Each of the nine en suite rooms is different; all are stylish, individual and memorable. The interior decoration includes mock-Byzantine frescoes, heavy carved wooden furniture and antique rugs.

The exterior is a lovely combination of white plaster and exposed stone, and there is a delightful café terrace paved with flagstones, from where you can admire the breathtaking panorama of Volos and the Gulf of Volos. Breakfast, coffee, cocktails and an imaginative assortment of *mezedhes* are served out here. The Karamarli is very professionally run, and although it is far from cheap, its attention to detail and high standards of service represent value for money.

∽

NEARBY Volos; E coast Pilion beaches; Mt Pilion ski slopes.
LOCATION Makrinitsa village
FOOD breakfast, snacks
PRICE €€€€
ROOMS 9 double with en suite WC and shower; all rooms have TV
FACILITIES café terrace
CREDIT CARDS AE, DC, MC, V
CHILDREN accepted
DISABLED not suitable
PETS not accepted
CLOSED never
PROPRIETORS Karamarli family

MAGNESIA

MAKRINITSA, PILION

ARCHONTIKO REPANA

TRADITIONAL INN

37011 Makrinitsa, Pilion
TEL 0428 99435 **FAX** 0428 99548

SET ABOVE THE MAIN STREET, this typical Pilion mansion is reached by walk-ing up a steep cobbled ramp, with a barred wooden gate leading into its shaded courtyard, where white iron chairs and marble-topped tables sit amid pots of roses and splashes of greenery. The Repana family's mansion is larger than some in the village, with seven bedrooms, and is decorated in the characteristic style of the Pilion region, with much dark wood and a multi-windowed, cantilevered upper storey beneath heavy stone slates, and stencilled patterns brightening up its brilliant whitewashed exterior.

There are excellent views of the Gulf of Volos and the heavily forested mountain slopes of Pilion, and although Makrinitsa is the most visited of all the picturesque Pilion villages it is quiet in the evening. The Archontiko Repana is popular with Greek and foreign visitors at all times of year and booking is essential. It is also advisable to tell the inn when you plan to arrive, as it is not staffed on a 24-hour basis.

The Repana (and its neighbour, O Theophilous) have the merit of being easy to find, making both a useful choice for your first night in Pilion. Many of the other Pilion mansion-inns are tucked away and annoyingly difficult to locate on first arriving.

NEARBY Pilion; ski slopes; beaches.
LOCATION on pedestrian main street of village, 150 m from car park
FOOD breakfast
PRICE ©©©
ROOMS 7 double
FACILITIES breakfast room, courtyard café
CREDIT CARDS not accepted
CHILDREN accepted
DISABLED not suitable
PETS not accepted
CLOSED never
PROPRIETOR Dimitra Repana

MAGNESIA

MAKRINITSA, PILION

O THEOPHILOUS
~ TRADITIONAL INN ~

37011 Makrinitsa, Pilion
TEL 0421 99435

A SHORT WALK FROM THE CAR PARK, above a narrow cobbled street in Makrinitsa, the closest of all the pretty Pilion villages to Volos, Theophilous is certainly the most conveniently located of all the remarkably attractive Pilion inns.

It is built in the traditional style of the region, with a wooden third storey jutting out above two white-painted lower floors, and with typical details such as stencilled patterns below the eaves and panes of coloured glass set into the walls above the top-floor windows.

Inside, the entire bulding – again typical of the region – makes much use of hardwood, with polished floors, panelled ceilings and wooden stairs. Outside the front door a narrow terrace above street level is crammed with flowering plants in pots; and in the reception and the adjoining parlour there are goat skins on the wooden floor, and an array of goat bells hanging above the kitchen. Wooden stairs lead to two small rooms on the second floor and three doubles on the third, sharing a sitting area with TV and a wooden balcony with awesome views over the Gulf of Volos and wonderful sunsets. The sitting area is decorated with old brass and copper lamps, red and gold icons, and local pottery. Do not expect this to be a full service hostelry. Apart from at breakfast time, staff are often absent.

~

NEARBY Volos; Mt Pilion ski slopes; beaches.
LOCATION 100 m from car park on main street of village
FOOD breakfast
PRICE €€€
ROOMS 5; 3 double, 2 single
FACILITIES parlour
CREDIT CARDS not accepted
CHILDREN not accepted
DISABLED not suitable
PETS never
CLOSED never
MANAGER Nikolaou Adam

MAGNESIA

PALAIO STADHMOS

~ TRADITIONAL INN ~

31010 Milies, Pilion
TEL 0423 68425 **FAX** 0423 86736

THIS TRADITIONAL STONE-BUILT HOTEL (with exposed woodwork rather than the usual Pilion white plaster, giving it a mellow appearance) stands next to the tiny terminus of the old narrow-gauge Pilion railway. Its miniature steam trains still run between Milies and Lexonia, on the coast, at weekends and the trip is fun.

The inn is surrounded by huge plane trees, and is very quiet, with the sound of birdsong and tiny streams all around. It is a family-run operation, and the accommodation side of the business is less important than the restaurant, which has more than 30 tables on terraces above the hotel and across the street. Its kitchen exudes wonderful cooking smells at lunch and dinner time, and its casseroles and savoury pies attract a clientele from as far away as Volos.

The hotel was among the first old Pilion buildings to be converted into an inn (in 1978) and is run with friendly efficiency by the Gouliotis family. It makes an ideal base for a couple of nights, or longer if what you want is peace. All it really lacks is a view, but the lovely wooded surroundings help to make up for that.

~

NEARBY Milies village; Pilion railway; Vizitsa; Koropi and Kala Nera beaches.
LOCATION 1 km from village centre
FOOD breakfast, lunch, dinner
PRICE €€
ROOMS 8 double with en suite WC and shower; all rooms have phone
FACILITIES restaurant
CREDIT CARDS MC, V
CHILDREN accepted
DISABLED not suitable
PETS not accepted
CLOSED never
PROPRIETOR Efstratios Gouliotis

MAGNESIA

MOURESSI, PILION

THE OLD SILK STORE
～ MANSION BED-AND-BREAKFAST ～

37001 Mouressi, Pilion
TEL 0426 49565 **FAX** 0426 49565

JILL SLEEMAN BOUGHT this pretty manor with its pale blue and yellow exterior, lush tropical garden and high ceilings to escape the madness of working in the package holiday business, and has restored it attractively and simply, with polished wood floors, rag rugs, and prints of old Greece on the walls. More than a century old, the mansion was used to store the raw silk produced by silkworms which were farmed here, feeding on the mulberry trees which grow around the village (Mouressi, in Greek, means something like 'Mulberryton').

The Old Silk Store's gardens extend all around the building and there are plenty of private nooks and corners, so there are places for peace and quiet even when the house is full. Grand marble steps lead from the garden to the front door, and a marble balcony juts from the second floor with breathtaking views of the sea and wooded slopes stretching down to Agios Ioannis beach below. The view is only slightly marred by the crudely functional but fortunately small concrete buildings opposite.

Jill leads half-day and longer walks through the glorious woods and villages of Pilion, linked by ancient cobbled mule paths, and for the energetic the beach is (just) within walking distance, though it is a steep climb back to the house.

～

NEARBY Tsangarada; Damouhari and Agios. Ioannis beaches; Pilion ski slopes.
LOCATION Mouressi village, above road
FOOD breakfast
PRICE €€€
ROOMS 4 twin, 1 studio cottage, 1 self-contained studio; 2 rooms, cottage and studio have en suite WC and shower, others have separate private bath
FACILITIES breakfast room, shared kitchenette, garden, courtyard
CREDIT CARDS MC, V
CHILDREN accepted
DISABLED not suitable
PETS not accepted
CLOSED Feb
PROPRIETOR Jill Sleeman

MAGNESIA

PORTARIA, PILION

HOTEL DESPOTIKO

~ TRADITIONAL MANSION ~

37011 Portaria, Pilion
TEL 0428 99046/01 722 7305

T HE VERY SUBSTANTIAL DESPOTIKO stands majestically in its own huge garden on the outskirts of Portaria village. The hotel comprises two wings – a newer, two-storey wing which has been so well designed to blend in that you would not guess it was a modern addition, and a huge, three-storey house dating from the 19th century with a slate roof, iron balconies on its top floor, and barred windows which give it a formidable look. Marble steps lead from the large garden to the front porch of this building, which is supported by stone columns which may well have come from some ancient Greek or Roman site.

The garden is a unique selling point for this hotel, as most Pilion inns have no more than a tiny courtyard. If you like plenty of space around you, this is the one to choose. The garden is very green and peaceful, with conifers and rose bushes, and the bedrooms are spacious and comfortably furnished.

Despotiko's only drawback is its awkward location. Local drivers manage to squeeze their way up the cobbled lanes to the square beside the hotel (under a huge plane tree with a gurgling fountain) but you may not wish to risk your paintwork; in which case it is a long, steep walk from the main road.

~

NEARBY Portaria; Volos; Pilion walks and ski slopes; beaches.
LOCATION 500 m from village centre
FOOD breakfast, snacks
PRICE €€€
ROOMS 21 double with en suite WC and shower; all rooms have phone, TV
FACILITIES sitting room, bar, garden
CREDIT CARDS DC
CHILDREN welcome
DISABLED not suitable
PETS accepted
CLOSED Jul-Sept
PROPRIETOR Anna Londou

MAGNESIA

PORTARIA, PILON

ARXONTIKO NAOUMIDI
~ TRADITIONAL MANSION ~

37011 Portaria, Pilion
TEL 0428 099470 **FAX** 0428 052600

THIS BEAUTIFUL, NEW, family-run addition to the Pilion portfolio opened in autumn 2001 and still smells of fresh paint and new polish. In a daring departure from local convention it is painted not white but rose pink, with slate-blue woodwork. Built in 1893, it has been completely refurbished (a venture which took the owners five years) and has been decorated with extreme attention to detail. The floors are polished wood, there are graceful plaster mouldings on the ceilings and painted dados on the walls, and the beds are genuine Greek antiques with brass and iron ends and decorative mirrorwork. Bathrooms are modern marble, with real bathtubs, and the bedrooms are furnished with a mixture of family antiques and reproduction furniture.

Downstairs, there is a stylishly furnished breakfast room where lavish breakfasts are served, a tiny bar, and a large paved courtyard under the shade of an enormous oak tree.

The Naoumidi is easy to find, on the main road through the village (no heavy traffic), and is next to the village car park. Families with younger children will find the village playground, with swings, roundabout and climbing frame, just a few steps away across a cobbled pedestrian lane.

~

NEARBY Makrinitsa; Pilion walks and ski slopes; beaches; Volos.
LOCATION village centre, beside car park and main road
FOOD breakfast
PRICE €€€
ROOMS 9 double, all with en suite WC and bath; all rooms have phone, TV, central heating
FACILITIES breakfast room, courtyard café
CREDIT CARDS MC, V
CHILDREN welcome
DISABLED not suitable
PETS accepted by arrangement
CLOSED never
PROPRIETORS Ilios Paxis - Anastasia Naoumi OE

MAGNESIA

TSANGARADA, PILION

KASTANIES

~ VILLAGE INN ~

37012 Tsangarada, Pilion
TEL 0426 49135 **FAX** 0426 49169

SET AMONG CHESTNUT and walnut trees, with a pretty patio crammed with pots of hydrangeas and pelargoniums, this very substantial mansion, with whitewashed walls and a massive slate roof, is in a tranquil spot looking out over the Aegean. It is a little hard to find so, when driving, you must watch carefully for the wooden arrows that lead you to it through the village.

Built in 1898, it has been lovingly restored, and the sitting room, breakfast room and bedrooms have been furnished and decorated with antiques from the family's own collection of local treasures. Carved wood and typical Pilion mural artwork feature prominently.

This is very much a family home, where guests really are treated as guests, and, while its location is not too convenient for the local *tavernas*, the personal touch definitely compensates – home-baked bread and more than a dozen different jams and preserves to choose from at breakfast time, for example. Perhaps not the ideal spot for a lengthy stay, but certainly a good choice for a night or two in Tsangarada while touring Pilion.

NEARBY Tsangarada; Damouhari and Agios Ioannis beaches; Pilion ski slopes.
LOCATION 1 km N of Tsangarada, above main road
FOOD breakfast
PRICE €€€
ROOMS 5; 4 double, 1 triple, all with en suite WC and shower; all rooms have phone, TV, minibar
FACILITIES garden
CREDIT CARDS MC, V
CHILDREN welcome
DISABLED not suitable
PETS accepted by arrangement
CLOSED never
PROPRIETOR Ioannis Siniosoglou

MAGNESIA

TSANGARADA, PILION

THE LOST UNICORN
~ VILLAGE INN ~

1 Staikos, Aghia Paraskevi, 37012 Tsangarada. Pilion
TEL 0426 49930 **FAX** 0426 49931

AT FIRST SIGHT, the Lost Unicorn is not the most prepossessing of Pilion hotels, despite its pretty garden terrace with a goldfish pond and its lovely location, just off one of Tsangarada's many church squares, under a 1,000-year-old plane tree. It is a modern, boxy, stone and concrete building, with no pretensions to grandeur.

Inside, however, is a unique and quirky inn, decorated and managed in a style that seems more suited to an English village than a Greek one, with heavy old furniture, brass curtain rails, decorative sabres and flintlock pistols hanging on the walls and a library and games room with comfy chairs and dark green walls. This is an inn with more character than most, and is well worth the effort taken to find it.

Rooms are comfortably furnished, with quilted coverlets and gauze curtains, and the hotel is conveniently located, not far from the main road and with several cafés and restaurants within easy walking distance. Only the very fit, however, will want to take the steep footpath that leads to Damouhari beach every day, and, as in most Pilion villages, your own transport is essential

NEARBY Damouhari and Agios Ioannis beaches.
LOCATION off Aghia Paraskevi church square in Tsangarada village
FOOD breakfast; lunch and dinner by arrangement
PRICE ©©©
ROOMS 10 with en-suite WC and shower; all rooms have phone, TV
FACILITIES sitting room, library/games room, bar, breakfast room
CREDIT CARDS not accepted
CHILDREN welcome
DISABLED not suitable
PETS not accepted
CLOSED never
PROPRIETOR Jan Busoff

MAGNESIA

TSANGARADA, PILION

THIMELI INN

~ TRADITIONAL INN ~

Sfetseika Agios Georgios, 37012 Tsangarada
TEL 0426 49595 **FAX** 0426 49595

INN IS STRETCHING THE DEFINITION a little, since this substantial, two-storey stone building, in an apple orchard some distance from the loosely defined 'centre' of Tsangarada, doesn't have a bar or restaurant, just a breakfast room and tables outside, where a massive, old-fashioned stone oven stands on a paved patio. This simple building, not as grand in design as some local mansions, is ideal for families or groups of friends, as it has only three rooms but can sleep up to 10 adults and children; it's more like staying in a French *gite* than a Greek hotel.

There is a single wooden balcony at the front of the building (with views of the sea), and the house is surrounded by apple and nut trees, with a tiny stream trickling – flowing is too energetic a word – over the terrace. Built in 1857, the house was restored in 1989 and is decorated inside with pretty Pilion textiles and wooden benches and chairs. Tsangarada is a quiet village, and Thimeli – almost 3 km off the main road through the village – is even more peaceful. If you want to walk up to the cafés and restaurants, however, steep stone paths offer a pedestrian-only shortcut. The only real snag is that Thimeli is too far from the sea for even the most energetic walker, so you will need a car when staying here.

~

NEARBY Tsangarada; Pilion ski slopes; beaches at Damouhari and Agios Ioannis.
LOCATION 3 km from village centre, below Tsangarada, 100 m from road
FOOD breakfast, self-catering
PRICE €€€
ROOMS 4; 3 double, 1 suite for 4, all with en suite WC and shower
FACILITIES garden
CREDIT CARDS not accepted
CHILDREN welcome
DISABLED not suitable
PETS accepted
CLOSED never
PROPRIETOR Sofia Kazakou

MAGNESIA

VIZITSA, PILION

ARXONTIKO BLANA

⟨∾ TRADITIONAL INN ∾⟩

37010 Vizitsa, Pilion
TEL 0423 86840 **FAX** 0423 22164

THIS FAMILY-OWNED MANSION, built in 1827, was restored in 1996 and is one of the most imposing houses in Vizitsa. Standing in a wide paved courtyard just above the church square, off a steep cobbled lane, the house has two sturdy lower storeys of plain, grey stone topped with an overhanging upper storey of white plaster and dark wood-framed windows with decorative detailing and coloured glass skylights. Inside, there's much carved wood panelling, polished wooden floors and dark furniture set off by bright striped textiles. On the top floor, which is brightly lit through its sunny windows and has fine views, there is a typical Pilion sitting area, with low wooden bench seats around a coffee table. The bedrooms are very comfortable, cosy and well equipped.

Arxontiko Blana has a large courtyard, where breakfast and coffee is served in summer under a slate-roofed pergola. It is also just a few steps from Vizitsa's lovely village square, which is shaded by gigantic plane trees and surrounded by cafés and *tavernas* and is a very pleasant place in which to spend an evening.

∾

NEARBY Milies village; Pilion railway; Vizitsa; Koropi and Kala Nera beaches.
LOCATION village centre
FOOD breakfast
PRICE €€€
ROOMS 5; 4 double with en suite WC and shower, 1 suite with en suite WC and whirlpool bath; all rooms have TV
FACILITIES courtyard
CREDIT CARDS not accepted
CHILDREN accepted
DISABLED not suitable
PETS accepted
CLOSED never
PROPRIETOR Dimitra Blana

MAGNESIA

VOLOS

HOTEL AEGLI AND PALLAS
∼ TOWN HOTEL ∼

Argonafton 24, 38333 Volos
TEL 0421 24471 **FAX** 0421 33006

THESE TWIN HISTORIC BUILDINGS are a unique blend of Art Deco and neo-classical architecture, located on the waterfront on a long, pedestrianized esplanade lined with palm trees and a mass of café terraces where the entire population of Volos seems to sit at night, with sailboats and motor cruisers moored alongside. Considering that it is close to the centre of a major provincial town, the Aegli (Pallas's Art Deco twin) is quiet and exudes charm. Next door Pallas, in neoclassical style, was being fully restored when we last visited and should have emerged as a brand new hotel inside a historic shell by the time this guide is published.

Built in 1932, the Aegli is immaculately kept up, but retains many attractive period touches. The rooms to the front of the building have fine views over the bay, although a little marred by the nearby commercial port. In the lobby, paintings of schooners and ocean liners recall Volos in its 19th and early 20th century heyday. The bedrooms are comfortable, with high ceilings and floor-to-ceiling windows with shutters and balconies, and are well equipped and neutrally but quite prettily furnished, with bedspreads and curtains in complementary coloured patterns.

∼

NEARBY Pilion villages; ski slopes; beaches.
LOCATION on waterfront 100 m from ferry port, close to town centre
FOOD breakfast
PRICE €€€
ROOMS 80; 72 twin, 8 suites, all with en suite WC and shower; all rooms have phone, TV, air conditioning
FACILITIES breakfast room, sitting area
CREDIT CARDS MC, V
CHILDREN accepted
DISABLED not suitable
PETS not accepted
CLOSED never
PROPRIETORS Hotel Aegli-Pallas SA

PHOKIDA

PENSION MARIA

~ VILLAGE GUESTHOUSE ~

Arahova
TEL 0267 31803

THIS ATMOSPHERIC little village pension would be the ideal place to stay for one or two nights when visiting the Delphi sights during low season. The front door opens on to a narrow, steep lane just a few steps from Arahova's main street and its *tavernas*. Inside is a vaulted lobby, with a clutter of antique wooden sofas with striped wool covers and small rush-seated chairs. The lobby opens into a high, daylit bar area with a wooden ceiling, natural rock walls, decorated with antiques and curios from wooden and brass tools and utensils to an ancient valve radio that sits behind the bar.

In one corner of the bar, a wooden staircase leads to the bedrooms. These are large, high-ceilinged rooms, full of traditional furnishings in dark wood with striped woollen blankets and sheepskin rugs, and, like the rest of the guesthouse, cosy and warm in winter and autumn, but pleasantly cool in summer.

Pension Maria has come to the attention of numerous guidebook and magazine writers, and is popular with Athenian winter visitors too, so booking well ahead is advisable.

~

NEARBY Arahova; Delphi; Mt Parnassos.
LOCATION village centre
FOOD breakfast
PRICE €€
ROOMS 7; 2 with en suite WC and shower
FACILITIES sitting room, bar
CREDIT CARDS not accepted
CHILDREN not suitable
DISABLED not suitable
PETS not accepted
CLOSED never
PROPRIETORS Giannis and Nikos Plitsos

PHOKIDA

HOTEL ACROPOLE
◇ VILLAGE HOTEL ◇

13 Filellinon, 33054 Delphi
TEL 0265 82675 **FAX** 0265 83171 **WEBISITE** www.delphi.com.gr

THIS WELCOMING, white-painted hotel with varnished pine woodwork, on a quiet street not far from Delphi's main attractions, is a pleasant surprise and has far more character than its attractive, but not particularly individual, exterior and stone-tiled sitting room might suggest.

The top-floor bedrooms have steeply sloping wood ceilings, in a cosy attic style. Beds and other furnishings are modern, in plain wood, and care has been taken in the choice of brightly-patterned curtains and bedcovers which brighten each room. But the big selling point is the million-dollar view from each balcony, looking down several hundred metres across the 'sea of olives' in the valley below, and out across the Gulf of Corinth.

This is far and away the most appealing place to stay in Delphi (which is notably short of hotels of character, as most visitors stay only one night). As it is only five minutes' walk from the ruins of ancient Delphi, it is an excellent base for exploring, and the substantial buffet breakfast will keep you going until dinner time. Owner Costas 'Babis' Kourelis is friendly, helpful and speaks good English, and his staff are equally amiable. The hotel's parking is especially useful since it is often hard to find a place to park on Delphi's narrow streets.

◇

NEARBY ancient Delphi; museum.
LOCATION 100 m from village centre, 500 m from archaeological site; car parking
FOOD buffet breakfast
PRICE €€€
ROOMS 40 double and twin with en suite WC and shower; all rooms have phone, TV, air conditioning, central heating, balcony
FACILITIES sitting room, bar, breakfast room
CREDIT CARDS AE, MC, V
CHILDREN accepted
DISABLED not suitable
PETS not accepted
CLOSED never
PROPRIETORS Costas and Socrates Kourelis

PHOKIDA

EPTALOFOS

ELATOS RESORT & HEALTH CLUB

~ MOUNTAIN RESORT ~

Eptalofos, Parnassos
TEL 0234 61162 **FAX** 0234 61161 **WEBSITE** www.elatos.com

HIGH ABOVE DELPHI and Arahova (1,300 m above sea level) on the slopes of Mt Parnassos, the Elatos Resort and Health Club is a collection of alpine-style log cabins surrounded by pine forests and awesome mountain scenery. The resort is aimed mainly at a well-off Athenian clientele, and, with its cool mountain breezes, is as much as 8°C cooler than the coast, making it an appealing place to escape from the worst of the summer heat. There is a wide range of leisure activities. The central building, which houses a restaurant, bar, sitting rooms and a café-terrace, is also in the style of an Alpine inn. The resort would make an ideal base for families wanting an active outdoors holiday away from the beach, or for those keen to explore the region by car, with ancient Delphi no more than 45 minutes' drive away.

Inside the chalets, the mountain theme continues, with varnished pine walls, ceiling and floor, sleeping galleries, and rugs woven in local patterns. Antiques and curios from the region, such as old brass goat bells, decorate the walls, and open fireplaces provide welcome warmth on chilly evenings.

~

NEARBY Mt Parnassos.
LOCATION 25 km N of Arahova, 8 km S of Eptalofos
FOOD breakfast, dinner, self-catering
PRICE €€€
ROOMS 40 wooden chalets sleeping 4-6; all chalets have kitchen, fireplace, verandah
FACILITIES sitting rooms, restaurant, bar, gym, sauna, indoor swimming pool, ski school, archery range
CREDIT CARDS not accepted
CHILDREN welcome
DISABLED not suitable
PETS accepted
CLOSED never
PROPRIETORS Elatos Resort & Health Club

PHOKIDA

GALAXIDI

HOTEL ARGO
~ VILLAGE HOTEL ~

33052 Galaxidi
TEL 0265 41996 **FAX** 0265 41291

THE NEOCLASSICAL Hotel Argo stands a short distance from the waterfront in the charming, quiet village of Galaxidi. An attractive neoclassical building, painted creamy white with blue shutters, it was once one of the sea-captain's houses for which the village is known, and is now a friendly, family-run hotel, with a tree-shaded garden and a bright and cheerful breakfast room, bar and reception area on the ground floor.

All the bedrooms are on the first floor, with high windows, plenty of daylight, and a muted colour scheme in neutral shades of slate blue and white, with pink soft furnishings, curtains and covers and newly tiled floors. Rooms at the front have balconies overlooking the garden, while those at the back look over the village and surrounding countryside.

The Argo is a value for money option for anyone looking for affordable, amiable accommodation within a short distance of the sights of Delphi (only half an hour away) but close to the sea. It serves breakfast, but for lunch or dinner there are plenty of commendable *tavernas* along the village quayside, including the fish restaurant O Tasos, under the same ownership as the hotel.

~

NEARBY Delphi.
LOCATION village centre
FOOD breakfast
PRICE €€
ROOMS 16 with en suite WC and shower; all rooms have phone, TV, air conditioning, balcony
FACILITIES sitting room, garden
CREDIT CARDS not accepted
CHILDREN accepted
DISABLED not suitable
PETS accepted by arrangement
CLOSED Nov-Mar
PROPRIETORS Hotel Argo SA

PHOKIDA

GALAXIDI

HOTEL ARXONTIKO

~ VILLAGE HOTEL ~

33052 Galaxidi
TEL 0265 42292 **FAX** 0265 41788

T HE HOTEL ARXONTIKO is a charming and colourful new arrival in Galaxidi, full of quirky character and run by an enthusiastic young couple who have put plenty of imagination into creating a captivating new place to stay. You enter the hotel along a path lined with Byzantine-style brick columns and decorated with pebble mosaics, through a newly planted garden which is still maturing but will be lovely within a year or so.

Each room is different (one has a round, pink double bed; another has a bed in the shape of a fishing boat; and the honeymoon suite has a canopied four-poster) and all have coffee-making facilities as well as a minibar. Upstairs rooms have a high pitched ceiling, and all have a private balcony or terrace with views of the Gulf of Corinth or the mountains.

On the ground floor, a café-bar and breakfast room open on to the garden and are furnished with old pine dressers and tables rescued from local homes. The owners are very friendly and eager to help, and the quiet location is an ideal spot to rest after a few days touring and seeing the sights. Galaxidi is the sort of place where you could happily spend a fortnight, but is also well placed en route between Delphi and Olympia and the sights of the Peloponnese.

~

NEARBY beach; harbour; Delphi.
LOCATION outskirts of Galaxidi, close to sea
FOOD breakfast
PRICE €€€
ROOMS 8 with en suite WC and shower; all rooms have phone, TV, air conditioning, minibar, coffee maker
FACILITIES breakfast room, garden
CREDIT CARDS not accepted
CHILDREN welcome
DISABLED not suitable
PETS not accepted
CLOSED never
PROPRIETORS Giannis and Argiroula Laiefa

PHOKIDA

HOTEL GALAXA
~ VILLAGE HOTEL ~

Eleftherias & Kennedy, Chirolakas, 33052 Galaxidi
TEL 0265 41620 **FAX** 0265 42053

THIS HOTEL IS A STRONG RIVAL to the nearby Ganimede for the title of 'best small hotel in Galaxidi'. It too is in an old sea-captain's house, this time set a little above the harbour on the west side of the village, with terrific views across the calm Gulf of Corinth to the mountains of the Peloponnese.

The rooms are spotless and, judging by the brilliant whiteness of their plastered walls, they must be repainted at least once a year. Woodwork, including shutters and window frames, is equally spotless and painted bright blue. Decoration and furnishings are delightfully simple, with wooden floors, striped rugs and wooden blanket chests in some rooms. The overall impression is of a family home; an impression borne out by the very friendly welcome offered by the owners Mr and Mrs Papillaris.

In summer, breakfast is served on a simple terrace overlooking the sea, with old-fashioned café tables and umbrellas. In cooler seasons, it is served in the original living room-kitchen of the house, a cosy room on the ground floor, with whitewashed walls, fireplace and a low wooden ceiling. To make things perfect, the Galaxa has its own caique, for day cruises along the Gulf of Corinth.

~

NEARBY Delphi; Arahova.
LOCATION Galaxidhi, overlooking harbour
FOOD breakfast
PRICE ©©©
ROOMS 10 double with en suite WC and shower; all rooms have air conditioning; 5 have sea-facing balcony
FACILITIES terrace
CREDIT CARDS not accepted
CHILDREN welcome
DISABLED not suitable **PETS** not accepted
CLOSED never
PROPRIETOR Emmanuel Papillaris

PHOKIDA

GALAXIDI

GANIMEDE HOTEL

~ VILLAGE HOTEL ~

33052 Galaxidi
TEL 0265 41328 **FAX** 0265 42160

THIS CHARMING PENSION, run by the ebullient Italian owner, is in a charming traditional sea-captain's house with architecture typical of this delightful little town just off the main highway along the north shore of the Gulf of Corinth. Galaxidi is so peaceful, you could easily be in the islands, and the Ganimede is a definite asset. Some rooms have coffered wooden ceilings painted in elaborate patterns, others are plain with wooden floors and rag rugs. Most look inward, over an attractive courtyard shaded from the summer sun by a canopy of vines, laburnum and wisteria, where breakfast is served at café tables each morning. This courtyard, with its small fountain, is also a lovely place to sit with a book and a coffee or cold drink in the heat of the day.

Brunello's breakfasts and evening aperitifs are excellent reasons for staying here, and the Ganimede is highly recommended as an overnight stop for those travelling by car between Delphi and Patras or Olympia. (There is plenty of car parking space on the street outside.) Given the dearth of hotels of distinction in Delphi (about 22 km away), it also makes a perfect base for those visiting the archaeological site there. One of the best small hotels we have discovered on the mainland.

~

NEARBY Delphi.
LOCATION centre of Galaxidi
FOOD breakfast, lunch, dinner
PRICE ⓔ
ROOMS 8 double or twin with en suite WC and shower
FACILITIES courtyard
CREDIT CARDS MC, V
CHILDREN welcome
DISABLED no access
PETS accepted
CLOSED Nov
PROPRIETOR S. Brunello

PHOKIDA

GALAXIDI

VILLA OLYMPIA

~ RESORT HOTEL ~

33052 Galaxidi
TEL 0265 41174 **FAX** 0265 41746

THE FIVE-STAR Villa Olympia, with its large pool, palm gardens, and low-rise elegance, would not look out of place on a Caribbean island. Instead, it is just outside the charming little fishing port of Galaxidi, on the Gulf of Corinth, with views across to the Peloponnese and the mountains of the northern mainland as a backdrop. All the rooms are large, at 45 square metres, with a wooden trellis separating the large double beds from the sitting area. Bathrooms are also spacious and have a full size tub. Every room has a verandah, with the best looking inward over the pool and lush tropical garden.

The colour scheme and decoration are quintessentially modern Greek, with some touches (such as the pink marble bathrooms in some rooms) a little on the ostentatious side. Furniture is also modern, mostly in wood veneer, and is not too florid in style. The rooms are very well equipped, making this a resort hotel with all the comfort one could wish for. The only puzzle is its location, as this is not a part of Greece known for five-star luxury resorts. Expect some traffic noise, as the hotel is close to a main road.

~

NEARBY Galaxidi; Delphi.
LOCATION 1.2 km from centre of Galaxidi, on main coast road
FOOD breakfast, lunch, dinner, snacks
PRICE €€€€
ROOMS 15 suites with double bed and sofa bed, en suite WC and bath; all rooms have phone, TV, minibar, verandah; one large apartment with 2 double bedrooms, sitting room, kitchen
FACILITIES 2 restaurants, bar, garden, swimming pool, pool bar,
CREDIT CARDS MC, V
CHILDREN welcome
DISABLED not suitable
PETS accepted
CLOSED never
MANAGER Gr. Siskos

ATTICA

ATHENS

ANDROMEDA HOTEL

~ CITY HOTEL ~

Timoleontas Vassou 22, 11521 Athens,
TEL 01 641 5000 **FAX** 01 646 6361
E-MAIL reservations@andromedaathens.gr

THE ANDROMEDA HOTEL is a real find. A small (but not too small), independently-owned boutique hotel, its location alone is a bonus in traffic saturated Athens, where finding a quiet small hotel is no easy task. The Andromeda is located on a quiet side street behind Plateia Mavillis, near the US Embassy and about 30 minutes' walk from Syntagma Square, the shops and restaurants of the Plaka and the sights of ancient Athens. The lobby area perhaps tries a little too hard to be opulent, with its pink marble and gold mirrors, but the combination of modern art objects and paintings with tastefully selected antiques and rugs is individual and interesting, and is carried through from public areas into the rooms, which are small but well appointed. A recent, slightly negative report suggests that some rooms are looking a little run-down and in need of redecoration. Service levels aim high, with laundry service and 24 hour room service. The à la carte restaurant is a little disappointing – it looks lovely, with lots of softly glowing wood panelling and low lighting, but its take on Oriental and what the menu calls 'Polynesian' cuisine fails to impress. Nevertheless, this small hotel is one of the very best bases for a stay in Athens.

NEARBY Plaka; Mt Lycabettos; Acropolis; Ancient Agora; Roman Agora; National Archaeological Museum.
LOCATION city centre
FOOD breakfast, lunch, dinner, 24 hr room service
PRICE ©©©©
ROOMS 30, all with WC/shower, TV, air conditioning, minibar
FACILITIES restaurant and bar
CREDIT CARDS AE, MC, V, DC
CHILDREN accepted
DISABLED adequate
PETS accepted
CLOSED never
PROPRIETORS Ambassador Hotel SA

MACEDONIA

PRESPA LAKES

AGIOS ACHILLIOS GUESTHOUSE

VILLAGE GUESTHOUSE

53077 Agios Achillios

TEL 0385 46601
FAX 0385 46112
FOOD breakfast, lunch, dinner
PRICE ©©© **CLOSED** never
PROPRIETOR Xenonas Agiou
Achilliou

A MODERN BUILDING in traditional style, with stone walls and pine woodwork, the Agios Achillios is remarkably located in the middle of the unique and newly created Prespa wildlife reserve, which embraces the huge inland lakes that cross the borders of Greece, Macedonia and Albania. They are a magnet for rare bird life including pelicans, storks and raptors. The downstairs bar and restaurant, with its wooden tables and chairs and mural painting of the lake, is a gathering place for locals as well as visitors, and serves fresh fish from the lake. Upstairs, all seven rooms have views of the lake, its reed beds, and the surrounding hills and forests. Service is friendly, and more attentive, than in many smaller guesthouses.

THESSALONIKI

REGENCY CLUB, HYATT REGENCY HOTEL

RESORT HOTEL

Km 13, Thessaloniki-Perea, 57001 Thessaloniki

TEL 031 401234 **FAX** 031 401100
E-MAIL hotel@hyatt..gr
PRICE ©©© **CLOSED** never
CREDIT CARDS MC, V

O NLY TWO MINUTES AWAY from Macedonia International Airport and a 15-minute drive from the sights and restaurants of downtown Thessaloniki, the Regency Club is an 80-room 'hotel within a hotel' and is part of the larger, 134-room Hyatt Regency Thessaloniki complex. Low-rise buildings are set among palm gardens and lily ponds, giving the Regency Club rooms (which have separate check-in area) the feel of a private oasis, which is why we break our rules on size to include them. And the pool is certainly the best in northern Greece; there is even an artificial waterfall. This would be an excellent base for anyone touring northern Greece by car, and especially families, as it is very child-friendly. It also has secure off-street parking, something no other Thessaloniki hotel offers.

MACEDONIA

THESSALONIKI

KRIKELAS

CITY RESTAURANT

Salaminos 6, 57001 Thessaloniki

TEL 031 050 1600
PRICE €€
CLOSED Sun
CREDIT CARDS MC, V

THE ORIGINAL KRIKELAS, at 32 Ethnikis Antistasseos has been a Thessaloniki landmark since 1940 and its new sister, housed in one of the recently converted warehouses in trendy Ladadika, outdoes the original for location and menu. Those familiar only with the tourist restaurants of the islands will be surprised by a menu which includes dishes typical of northern Greece, and appetisers such as salted tuna from Istanbul, smoked mullet, smoked eel and pastrami *poleos*. The main dishes have their accent on meat, and include baby lamb and suckling pig as house specialities. The menu also features a wide range of traditional desserts such as *halvah*, baked quince, and *kadaifi* as well as fruit, cakes and ice cream.

THESSALONIKI

TAVERNA-OUZERI 1901

CITY TAVERNA

Katouni 9, 57001 Thessaloniki

TEL 031 540 284
PRICE €€
CLOSED never
CREDIT CARDS AE, V

THE CAREFULLY RESTORED, pink, white and yellow stucco façade of Taverna-Ouzeri 1901, in two adjoining historic buildings, greets you as you enter the Ladadika district (heart of Thessaloniki's nightlife) from the city centre. The menu is traditional Thessaloniki, with plenty of typical appetizers, from *melitzanosalata* (aubergine dip) to pickled peppers and *poikilia*. Specialities of the house include the 1901 casserole, which serves two and is a dish for a cold winter evening, rather than a warm summer night. There is a wide selection of salads, cheeses and vegetarian dishes, and the wine list has an excellent choice of the new breed of varietal Greek wines from Boutari and other top-notch wine makers.

IOANNINA

ASTRAKA

VILLAGE GUESTHOUSE

44016 Megalo Papingo, Zagoria

TEL 0653 41693
FOOD breakfast, self-catering
PRICE €€
CLOSED never
CREDIT CARDS not accepted
PROPRIETOR Angeliki Kotsoridou

NAMED AFTER THE MOUNTAIN which looms over the delightful village, the Astraka occupies two sides of a stone-paved village square which is shaded by an immense plane tree. Some rooms are in solidly built grey stone mansion which stands in a flowery courtyard, others are in converted outbuildings beside what must once have been a stable yard, to one side of the square. All are simply furnished, with wooden platform beds and stone fireplaces. From the square and garden (though not from most rooms) there are excellent views. You may prepare your own breakfast or snacks in a shared kitchen, but breakfast is also served in the first-floor dining room of the main house, or in the courtyard outside.

HOTEL DRAKOLIMNI

VILLAGE HOTEL

44010 Tsepelovo, Zagoria

TEL 0653 81312 **FAX** 0653 81311
FOOD breakfast, lunch, dinner
PRICE €€€ **CLOSED** never
PROPRIETORS Hotel Drakolimni

IF YOU ARE looking for a full service hotel in the heart of the Zagoria region (where most accommodation is in small guesthouses or private homes), the Hotel Drakolimni is the one to choose. Just at the edge of Tsepelovo village, it shares the village's magnificent views. Although a new building, it has been sensitively designed and merges well with local styles, with the dove-grey masonry, heavy slate roof and wooden balconies typical of Zagoria mansions.

There is a wide open-air terrace with a dozen round metal café tables and canvas director's chairs, and a large open-plan reception, lobby and sitting area. The rooms are large, comfortable and well furnished. The Hotel Drakolimni also recommends itself to travellers without cars, as it has its own minibus and runs transfers from Ioannina airport, as well as daily excursions.

METSOVO

METSOVO

HOTEL EGNATIA

VILLAGE HOTEL

44200 Metsovo

TEL 0656 44200
Fax 0656 41485
FOOD breakfast, lunch, dinner
PRICE €€€ **CLOSED** Sun
PROPRIETORS Talaris brothers

WITH ITS PARADE OF FLAGS above the doorway, the Egnatia advertises itself as an international tourist hotel. We rate it as an attractive enough (and very comfortable) overnight stop in Metsovo, although its design and style are not distinguished. The lobby area is cool and shady in summer (and cosy in winter), with a stone floor and benches covered with bright, striped textiles. The rooms have carpeted floors (a departure from the traditional polished wood) and pine plank walls and ceilings, and are immaculately maintained, with the best views from the balconies of the top (third) floor. The Egnatia manages to be both friendly and very professionally managed.

EPIRUS

IOANNINA

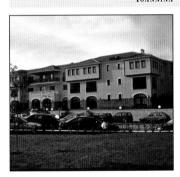

HOTEL DU LAC

TOWN HOTEL

Akti Miaouli and Ikkou, Ioannina

TEL 0651 22666
FAX 0651 22664
FOOD breakfast, lunch, dinner, snacks
PRICE €€€
CLOSED never
PROPRIETOR Hotel du Lac SA

ALTHOUGH THIS MODERN hotel (built in 1998) is larger than most others included in this book, it has been designed with careful attention to the traditional architecture of Ioannina and, with its pool and attractive gardens, is the most luxurious place to stay in the most attractive historic town in Epirus.

Overhanging balconies and an arcaded ground floor lend character to the building, and its lakeside location, facilities and a choice of bars and restaurants compensate for a slightly sterile atmosphere and run-of-the-mill service. Ask for a room with a view over the emerald Lake Pamvotis.

EPIRUS

IOANNINA

RESTAURANT O GRIPOS-PAMVOTIS

ISLAND RESTAURANT

Nisi, Lake Pamvotis, Ioannina

TEL 0651 81081
PRICE €€
CREDIT CARDS not accepted
CLOSED never

LAKE CARP, EELS, frogs and crayfish feature at these two restaurants side by side on the quayside of the little island in the middle of reed-fringed, pea-green Lake Pamvotis. It may be too much to assume that Lord Byron ate here, but he certainly visited the island when it was the seat of the 19thC potentate of Epirus, Ali Pasha, whose mansion on the island is now a museum. Pamvotis offers outdoor eating under the shade of a spreading plane tree and a slightly better view of the surrounding mountains. Menus and prices are more or less identical in both. Getting here (shuttle ferry boats from the lake front at Ioannina, run about every half an hour and take 15 minutes) is half the fun. You won't find food like this in many other places in Greece, but for the less adventurous, there are more simple dishes too.

MAGNESIA

VIZITSA, PILION

XENONAS THETIS

VILLAGE GUESTHOUSE

31010 Vizitsa, Pilion

TEL 0651 22666
FOOD breakfast
PRICE €€
CLOSED never
MANAGER Ekaterina Kaneliou

NEXT TO THE GRAND BLANA, the Thetis is smaller, cosy, and styles itself as a 'guesthouse' rather than a 'mansion'. It has traditional decorative details, such as stencilled wall paintwork, and warm rugs soften its wooden floors. The eight bedrooms are equally warm and unpretentious, and are furnished, as are the public areas, with traditional wooden furniture.

Xenonas Thetis also has its own tiny café, in a slate-roofed building in the courtyard of the main house, where you can eat indoors in winter and outdoors on the terrace under plane trees in the summer. All in all, a delightful little place for a few nights, though perhaps not for much longer.

PHOKIDA

ARAHOVA

GHENERALI
VILLAGE GUESTHOUSE

Roloi, Arahova

TEL 0267 31259
FAX 0267 32287
FOOD breakfast, dinner to order, self-catering
PRICE ⅲ
CLOSED Jul-Aug
PROPRIETOR K. Stamatis

THIS HARD-TO-FIND village guesthouse is worth the effort. Ghenerali is just below the church in the part of Arahova overlooked by the village clock-tower; walk down the steps to the church, turn left, and walk another 50 m down a steep lane to the mellow, ochre-covered building with deep eaves and logs piled ready for winter on its wooden balconies. This is very much a family home, and you will be made to feel extremely welcome, while the six individually decorated studios are charming and comfortable, with modern amenities. The 'Helicopter' studio has the best view of the mountains and the valley towards Delphi. Ghenerali is especially popular with Athenian visitors in autumn and winter, so you need to book well ahead for these times.

ARAHOVA

HOTEL LYKOREIA
VILLAGE HOTEL

Arahova

TEL 0267 31180
FAX 0267 32132
PRICE €€
FOOD breakfast, snacks
CLOSED Jul-Aug
PROPRIETORS Ioanna Perveli

THE LYKOREIA IS A COSY LOCAL MEETING PLACE with an agreeable café-bar much frequented by regulars and often alive with the clatter of backgammon games, which seem to interest the clientele more than the fantastic view from the sitting room. Floors in the public areas are stone tiled, with pretty rugs in traditional patterns, and the rooms are cosy, some with large double beds, others with twin beds. The view from the rooms facing south and west down the valley (rooms 40-47 in particular) is stupendous.

Arahova has much more character and a much greater choice of eating places than neighbouring Delphi (only five minutes' drive away), and the Lykoreia would be a very pleasant place to stay before or after a visit to the ruins of ancient Delphi.

PHOKIDA

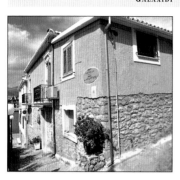

PENSION VOTSALO

VILLAGE GUESTHOUSE

33052 Galaxidi

TEL 0265 41788
FOOD none
PRICE €€
CREDIT CARDS not accepted
PROPRIETORS Giannis and Argiroula Laiefa

GIANNIS AND ARGIROULA LAIEFA, proprietors of the delightful Hotel Arxontiko (see page 81), also own this pretty little pension in the centre of Galaxidi, just above the sea and reached by a set of narrow steps with black and white pebble mosaics. Its ochre walls are set off by lavender blue woodwork, and there are fine decorative touches such as wrought-iron balconies with decorative figures and neoclassical stucco cameos above each window.

The Votsalo is in a very quiet location (even during the day you can hear the water lapping and the cicadas singing) and has just three simple bedrooms, all plainly but charmingly decorated and equipped with air conditioning and coffee making facilities.

OMILOS

HARBOURSIDE RESTAURANT

Galaxidi

PRICE €€
CREDIT CARDS MC, V
CLOSED Jan-Feb

WHICH OF GALAXIDI'S many fish restaurants should you choose? The Omilos has the advantage of its own private bathing pier (with sun loungers and umbrellas) where harassed parents can banish children and digest lunch in peace. Blue and white tables stand under an awning on a private jetty which juts into the harbour, with fishing boats moored alongside. Simple fish dishes are well prepared and fresh, but expect to wait a while when the place is busy (sometimes you could even fit in a quick swim between courses). Altogether, one of the best spots to linger over lunch or dinner, with shoals of fish splashing in the clear water beside your table and lovely surroundings.

ATTICA

ACROPOLIS HOUSE

CITYHOTEL

6-8 Kodrou and Voulis, Plaka, Athens

TEL 01 322 2344
FAX 01 322 6241
FOOD breakfast
PRICE €€
CLOSED never
PROPRIETOR Evridiki Houdalakis

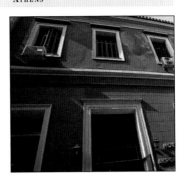

YOU ENTER THIS SMALL HOTEL, in the heart of the historic Plaka district, through a little lobby with attractive wall and ceiling paintings. A government designated landmark building, this 19thC mansion has been run as a hotel by the Houdalakis family since 1965. Rooms are comfortable, well appointed, and quiet by Plaka standards, but with neutral furnishings and decorations and less character than the lobby might suggest. The cheaper rooms are on the small side. Close to most of the best known archaeological sites and museums, Acropolis House is, all in all, a good base for a stay in the Plaka, offering comfort and value for money, but not a hotel to linger in.

ART GALLERY HOTEL

CITY HOTEL

5 Erechthion

TEL 01 923 8376
FAX 01 923 3025
FOOD breakfast
PRICE €€
CLOSED never
PROPRIETORS AssimAcopoulos family

THIS SMALL, UNPRETENTIOUS hotel on the edge of the Makrigianni district is conveniently located for the main sights but a little distance from the busiest streets and late-night noise of the Plaka. Its Greek-Canadian owner-managers are friendly and helpful (one useful facility for the first-time visitor to Greece is the small library of guidebooks kept in the reception area), and the rooms have ceiling fans and polished hardwood floors. Some rooms are decorated with original works of art. Certainly not for those looking for a luxury hotel, but ideal for the visitor on a modest budget, who wants a base for a couple of nights close to the historic sights and museums. There are rooms with three or four beds.

ATTICA

ATHENS

DAPHNE'S
CITY RESTAURANT

4 Lysikratous

TEL 01 322 7971
PRICE €€€€
CLOSED never
CREDIT CARDS AE, DC, MC, V

IF YOU HAVE TIME to visit only one restaurant during your stay in Athens it should be Daphne's. French President Valéry Giscard d'Estaing and Hilary Rodham Clinton are among the movers and shakers who have left written testimonials to the 'nouvelle Greek' cooking and luxurious atmosphere of this grand city restaurant. Imaginative dishes include rabbit in Mavrodaphne sauce and veal with quince. Tables are much in demand, and reservations are essential.

Close to the new Acropolis metro station, Daphne's is in an immaculately restored 19thC town house, decorated with gorgeous, richly coloured frescoes, and the best tables are in a delightful inner courtyard.

ATHENS

JOHN'S HOTEL
CITY HOTEL

Pandoras 3 & Lazaraki, 16674 Glyfada, Athens

TEL 01 894 6837/9
FAX 01 898 0210
FOOD breakfast, lunch, dinner
PRICE €€€
CLOSED never
PROPRIETORS John's SA

THIS SMALL, MODERN, medium-rise hotel in the well-off Glyfada suburb of Athens used to be ideal for those arriving late or leaving early from the old airport, which was conveniently situated just five minutes away. The new airport, at Spata, is around 30 minutes away. John's, however, is still excellent value for those who want a small hotel in a quiet location outside the city centre.

It has an attractive bar and foyer, decorated in a style that one recent visitor found a little reminiscent of Miami Art Deco. Service is cool but professional, and a terrace with palm trees and garden with a 15-m (50-ft) pool are real bonuses.

ATTICA

ATHENS

KEFALARI SUITES

CITY HOTEL

1 Pendelis/Kolokotronis, Kifissia, Athens

TEL 01 623 3333
FAX 01 623 3330
FOOD breakfast
PRICE €€€€€ **CLOSED** never
PROPRIETORS Kefalari SA

IN ONE OF THE CAPITAL'S most sought-after suburbs, this neoclassical-style hotel is an exceptionally relaxing place to stay. It is small enough to feel intimate, and far enough from the busy city centre to be comfortably quiet even in high season. Each of the 12 self-contained, well-appointed suites has a small kitchen area, and each is individually and attractively decorated, with old prints and furniture upholstered to match the canopied beds. This is not a full-service hotel, but would be ideal for the visitor looking for a home away from home for a longer stay in Athens. There is a small reception area, but for eating and drinking you must seek out one of Kifissia's many restaurants (try the Pentelikonís restaurant, nearby).

ATHENS

MARBLE HOUSE INN

CITY GUESTHOUSE

Zinni Anastasiou 35, 11471 Athens
TEL 01 923 4058 **FAX** 01 922 6461
FOOD breakfast **PRICE** €
CLOSED never
PROPRIETORS Marble House Inn

FRIENDLY, EFFICIENT, AFFORDABLE and family run, Marble House Inn is located in a quiet side street off one of the capital's main boulevards. If your budget is tight, it is a handy place to stay for just one night on your way through Athens and it earns its place in this edition mainly because it offers good value for money. The functional design of the exterior is softened by extensive greenery, and the rooms, though spartan, are clean and well kept.

On the downside, the stairs and corridors echo noisily at night, and rooms have no sound insulation. Since many of its younger guests stay out until the earlier hours, this can interfere with a good night's sleep. To compensate, the south-west facing balconies shared between rooms at the front are pleasant places to sit in the afternoon or evening.

SOUTHERN MAINLAND

AREA INTRODUCTION

SOUTHERN GREECE IS A REGION APART, and its delights have yet to be discovered by large numbers of foreign visitors. Those delights include the wonderful classical and Hellenistic ruins of Olympia and Corinth, the even more ancient remnants of Agamemnon's Mycenae and Nestor's Pylos; the mighty Venetian fortresses of Methoni and Koroni; the Byzantine strongholds or Mistras and Monemvasia, and the hilltop castles of Frankish barons and Turkish pashas.

The Peloponnese region (embracing all of the south) is separated from the northern mainland by the Gulf of Corinth, and is lapped by the Ionian, Mediterranean and Aegean seas, with the massive, saw-toothed *cordillera* of the Taigetos range forming its backbone. There are some fine long, sandy beaches (surprisingly little developed by the tourism industry) on its western, or Ionian coast, and tiny, undiscovered coves are dotted at intervals along the precipitous Aegean coast. To the south, the Mani peninsula terminates at Cape Tainaron (or Matapan), the southernmost point of mainland Europe.

Greece's third largest town, Patras (the gateway to Greece for those arriving by ferry from Italy) is close to the region's northwest corner, and Corinth straddles its eponymous Isthmus at the east end of the Gulf. Athens, with its international airport, is around two hours' drive from Corinth, and there are charter flights in summer to Kalamata, on the south coast.

Most of our favourite hotels in this idyllic part of Greece are on or near the coast, but we have also found a few in delightful mountain villages, as well as some acceptable candidates in key locations close to the most important sights, such as Olympia, Mycenae and Mistras.

The Mani peninsula, undiscovered by tourism as recently as the mid-1980s, makes an especially strong showing. Many of its characteristic clan towers have been converted into comfortable, mainly family-run guest-houses and are delightful, individual places to stay. Also outstanding is the fortified ghost city of Monemvasia, with some of the most charming small hotels in mainland Greece. The very attractive little port of Navplio, with its streets of neoclassical town houses dating from a brief 19thC heyday as independent Greece's first capital, also gets an honourable mention.

Summer comes earlier to the south, and lingers longer, making this region ideal if you seek early or last-minute sunshine. You can swim and sunbathe as late as October, and early spring is a good time for a touring holiday, but December-February is best avoided, and July and August can be very hot indeed.

AHAIA

PATRAS

PRIMAROLIA ART HOTEL

~ CITY HOTEL ~

33 Othono Amalias, Patras
TEL 061 240 740 **FAX** 061 623 559 **WEBSITE** www.arthotel.gr

THE UNUSUAL, QUIRKILY STYLISH Primarolia Art Hotel is a welcome newcomer to the hotel scene in southern Greece's largest city. Well off the main tourist beat, Patras seems an unlikely setting for this 'boutique hotel', with its neoclassical façade, full-length glass windows and doors on the ground floor, and rooms boasting upmarket modern facilities, such as internet access, fax, computer on request, cigar humidor and Jacuzzi.

The lobby and the individually decorated rooms display art and design by world famous names such as Arne Jacobson and Mies van der Rohe. The paintings are by some of Greece's best-known painters, and the floors are made of Japanese hardwood and embellished by collector's carpets from Iraq and northern Iran. In the restaurant, fresh local ingredients dominate an imaginative menu and the wine list combines Achaian and New World vintages.

If this hotel were in a more fashionable city than Patras, it would already have an international reputation. It certainly deserves full marks for bringing new levels of style and service to this part of Greece.

~

NEARBY ancient Olympia; Kalavrita railway; beaches at Killini.
LOCATION central Patras, 6 km from airport; car parking
FOOD breakfast, lunch, dinner; room service
PRICE ©©©©
ROOMS 14 single, double and executive suites, all with en suite bath; all rooms have phone, TV, video, air conditioning, minibar, hairdrier
FACILITIES bar, restaurant, business desk, lift
CREDIT CARDS AE, DC, MC, V
CHILDREN not suitable
DISABLED access possible
PETS accepted
CLOSED never
PROPRIETORS Primarolia SA

ARCADIA

OLYMPIA

HOTEL EUROPA OLYMPIA

~ COUNTRYSIDE RESORT ~

27965 Ancient Olympia
TEL 0624 22650 **FAX** 0624 23166

ALTHOUGH THE HOTEL EUROPA is part of the worldwide Best Western hotel consortium, it is family-managed and certainly does not feel like a chain hotel. It is set between modern Olympia and the ancient ruins (which are within walking distance), on a hillside among vineyards, olive groves and gentle, fertile countryside.

The lobby is attractively designed, with floor-to-ceiling windows, and has a flagstone floor. The well-furnished rooms are in wings leading off the main building, and the view and location more than make up for any lack of character. Some rooms are split-level, with the bed on a lower level.

The restaurant, which has panoramic views, is the best in Olympia, with a menu which features locally grown and organic produce. The gardens are lush and well laid out, surrounding a full-sized swimming pool. In short, there is no doubt that the Europe is by far the best place to stay when visiting Olympia, and not only does it have all the amenities, but it is also reasonably priced. '*Et in Arcadia ego*', to quote the poet.

~

NEARBY Ancient Olympia.
LOCATION midway between archaeological site and new town; car parking
FOOD breakfast, lunch, dinner
PRICE €€€
ROOMS 44; 42 double, 2 suites, all with en suite WC and shower; all rooms have phone, TV, air conditioning
FACILITIES café, bar, restaurant, terrace, garden, swimming pool, tennis court
CREDIT CARDS AE, MC, V
CHILDREN welcome
DISABLED access possible
PETS accepted by arrangement
CLOSED never
PROPRIETORS Best Western Hotel Europa

LAKONIA

NAFPLION

HOTEL BYRON

~ TOWN HOTEL ~

Platanos 2, 21100 Nafplion
TEL 0752 22351 **FAX** 0752 26338

IT IS WORTH MAKING A DETOUR to the pretty little port of Nafplion just to spend a night or two in this delightful small hotel. Housed in traditional buildings in a street below the 11thC Venetian fortress and painted pink with pale-blue woodwork and shutters, the Byron looks charming from the outside. The rooms are simple but very pretty and immaculately maintained, with polished wooden floors, painted shutters and some authentic, traditional antique furniture.

Most of the rooms have fine views over the pantiled roofs of the old town and out over the bay and some have sunny private terraces. The Byron also has a very attractive café terrace on the ground floor, for breakfast, snacks and afternoon ice-cream or evening drinks. The hotel is managed by its owner and the large number of guests who return again and again is a tribute to his professionalism. For once (and all too rarely) the standards of service match the good looks of this 'boutique hotel'.

Sadly, there is no evidence that Lord Byron ever stayed here during his sojourns in Greece, but it is certainly romantic enough to have satisfied him. The Byron is an excellent base from which to explore the sights of the Argolid, including ancient Mycenae.

~

NEARBY Palamidi fortress; Mycenae; Tiryns; Epidavros.
LOCATION in an upper street of the old town
FOOD breakfast, snacks
PRICE €€€
ROOMS 17 double with en suite WC and shower
FACILITIES café terrace
CREDIT CARDS AE, MC, V
CHILDREN accepted
DISABLED not suitable
PETS accepted by arrangement
CLOSED never
PROPRIETOR Aris Babaioannou

ARGOLIS

OMORFO POLI

~ TOWN HOTEL ~

Sofroni 5, 21100 Nafplion
TEL and **FAX** 0752 21565

THIS OLD NEOCLASSICAL town house, painted a warm rose-pink with white details, is on a narrow street not far from the harbour in one of Greece's prettiest old towns. On the ground floor is a cheerful café-bar which is a rather self-conscious retro recreation of an old-fashioned Greek café, decorated with 1950s posters and ephemera. Upstairs, each room is different, but all are considerably more stylish and luxurious than you might expect from the building's attractive but unassuming exterior. They have tiled or polished wood floors, high ceilings, tall shuttered windows and old-fashioned iron and brass double beds. The price is right, too. All things considered, a useful address for a stay of several nights when exploring this part of Greece.

~

NEARBY harbour; Venetian fortress; archaeological sites at Mycenae; Tiryns; Argos.
LOCATION town centre
FOOD breakfast, snacks
PRICE €€€
ROOMS 9 double or twin, each with en suite shower and WC
FACILITIES café-bar
CREDIT CARDS V
CHILDREN not suitable
DISABLED not suitable
PETS not suitable
CLOSED never
PROPRIETORS Omorfo Poli SA

LAKONIA

AREOPOLI, MANI

HOTEL KASTRO MAINI
~ TOWN HOTEL ~

23062 Areopoli, Mani, Lakonia
TEL 0733 51238 **FAX** 0733 29514

THE HOTEL KASTRO MAINI is a brand new, two-storey building among stony fields, a few hundred metres from the centre of Areopoli. Its grounds are still maturing (some of the palm trees are still only a couple of feet high) but will soon be very attractive. The hotel has been designed with a nod to local architectural style: it is built in local stone, with arches along the front of the building sheltering wooden tables and chairs. Be sure to ask for a room at the back of the hotel. These have superb sunset views; the rooms at the front look out over the drab concrete roof of the ground-floor reception area to rather unattractive modern buildings.

The tiled lobby, reception and breakfast room has natural stone walls, with a fireplace nook beside the bar which is a cosy place to sit with an evening drink in the cooler months of the year. A marble staircase leads to bedrooms on the upper floor, which are modern and neutral, with marble bathrooms and marble-topped dressing tables. Arguably, this new property has less character than some of its local competitors, but its modern comforts (among them, one of only three swimming pools in the entire region) help to compensate.

~

NEARBY Areopoli; Dirou caves; Mani villages; Passava and Kelefa castles.
LOCATION outskirts of Areopoli village, close to main road
FOOD breakfast, snacks
PRICE €€€
ROOMS 29 suites, all with WC and shower
FACILITIES sitting area, breakfast room, bar, café, swimming pool
CREDIT CARDS MC, V
CHILDREN welcome
DISABLED access difficult
PETS by arrangement
CLOSED never
PROPRIETOR Goudis Evstratios

LAKONIA

AREOPOLI, MANI

TSIMOVA GUESTHOUSE

~ VILLAGE GUESTHOUSE ~

23062 Areopoli, Lakonia
TEL 0733 51013

CAST-IRON CANNON and crouching lions guard the arched doorway of this little stone tower house on a church square in the centre of Areopoli, largest village in the Mani (formerly called Tsimova, until renamed after playing a starring role in the War of Independence which began here in 1821). Flowering shrubs in pots soften the tower's square outline. It was built in 1870, and owner Georgios Versakos, a veteran of the Second World World War resistance, celebrates Mani's turbulent history with his own 'private war museum'. Inside his sturdy family home, one large, stone-floored living room occupies the entire ground floor, its walls hung with glass cases stuffed with daggers, scimitars, bayonets, muskets, flintlock pistols, machine guns and other tools of destruction.

If you speak any Greek, Georgios will regale you with tales of the resistance. The place certainly has plenty of character. Upstairs, the wooden floored, stone-walled rooms have traditional furniture and look out over the square and village rooftops to the surrounding mountains. Areopoli has a bigger choice of places in which to eat and drink than the other even smaller Mani villages and makes a good base for exploring the area.

~

NEARBY Passava castle; Kelefa castle; other Mani villages; Dirou caves.
LOCATION village centre
FOOD breakfast
PRICE €€
ROOMS; 6 double, all with WC and shower
CREDIT CARDS not accepted
CHILDREN accepted
DISABLED not suitable
PETS by arrangement
CLOSED Nov-Mar
PROPRIETOR Georgios Versakos

LAKONIA

AREOPOLI

XENONAS LONDAS

~ TOWER GUESTHOUSE ~

23062 Areopoli, Lakonia
TEL 0733 51012 **FAX** 0733 51360 **E-MAIL** londas@otenet.gr

LONDAS WAS ONE of the very first of the Maniot tower houses to be restored as a place to stay, and has been in business since 1988. These remarkable miniature castles are steeped in the unique (and bloody) heritage of the Mani, a land of fiercely independent clans often locked in generations-long vendettas. Fortunately, little sense of this harsh history lingers here, though it was once the seat of one of the greatest of all the clans, the Mavromichalis family, who built the tower in 1798 and marched from this stronghold to begin Greece's War of Independence in 1821.

The four-square stone tower has a vaulted sitting room and dining room on the ground floor, and four luxurious bedrooms, reached by marble stairs, on the upper storeys. Sunny private terraces have views across the rooftops of Areopolis to the treeless hills of the Deep Mani and the olive groves which surround the village. Rooms and public areas are graced by local antiques from the owner's own collection, though most of the furnishings are modern.

Breakfast is a treat, with home-made cheese, honey, jams and locally grown fruit, and there are recommended *tavernas* within walking distance in Areopolis village.

~

NEARBY Passava and Tigani castles; Mani villages.
LOCATION Areopolis village centre
FOOD breakfast
PRICE €€
ROOMS 4 double with en suite WC and shower
FACILITIES sitting room
CREDIT CARDS MC, V
CHILDREN accepted
DISABLED not suitable
PETS welcome
CLOSED never
PROPRIETOR Iakovos Xenakis

LAKONIA

ITILO, MANI

ALEVRA'S TOWER
～ FAMILY GUESTHOUSE ～

23062 Itilo, Mani
TEL 0733 59388 **FAX** 0733 51802

T HE VIEW IS THE MOST IMMEDIATELY IMPRESSIVE aspect of this small, family-run guesthouse, perched a few hundred metres above a small village which is hardly touched by tourism. To the north and west are steep hill-sides and barren mountains; to the south and east are the sheltered bay of Itilo and the steep ravine guarded by the ruins of Kelefa castle. The square stone tower is charmingly adorned with little design details such as carved rosettes and other ornamentation around the front door; a little earthen-ware mermaid on the steps to the pool; and pottery shells and decorations set into the stonework of the balconies outside some of the rooms.

The bedrooms are neutral in style, with marble floors and modern fur-niture. Three of the rooms have private balconies with great views; but it has to be said that the two smaller rooms are not nearly as attractive. Compensating for this is the fair-sized swimming pool, which also makes up for Alevra's location, high above the sea, which seems enticingly close but is just too far away to reach without a car. Owner Nikos Alevras is a well-known Greek documentary film-maker, and Alevra's Tower is friendly and well managed.

～

NEARBY Itilo; Kelefa castle; Areopoli; Dirou caves.
LOCATION above Itilo village centre
FOOD breakfast
PRICE €€€
ROOMS; 15 double, all have shower and WC, air conditioning; three have kitchenette
FACILITIES swimming pool, garden
CREDIT CARDS not accepted
CHILDREN welcome
DISABLED not suitable
PETS by arrangement
CLOSED Oct-Mar
PROPRIETOR Nikos Alevras

LAKONIA

MONEMVASIA

ARDAMIS

～ TRADITIONAL VILLAGE APARTMENTS ～

23070 Kastro , Monemvasia, Lakonia
TEL 0732 61886 **FAX** 0732 233532

IN AN OLD STONE BUILDING inside the tall Kastro walls, hidden behind an arched gateway, the Ardamis apartments are a well-kept secret. There are only four apartments and they are much in demand from a loyal clientele, so booking early is essential. Alternatively, visit Monemvasia off-season, between Easter and early June, or in October. It is well worth the effort; the apartments are roomy, with high wooden ceilings, thick wool rugs on the floor, and simple but elegant traditional-style wooden beds, dressers and chairs. Bathrooms are in marble, and rooms are graced by antique carvings and old earthenware pottery.

The Ardamis does not provide a full service, but coffee and drinks are available in the pretty courtyard. Apartments are fully equipped for self-catering, and there are half a dozen café-bars and restaurants within a few hundred metres.

Monemvasia has no beach, but the Ardamis rooms and terrace face out to sea, with the sea-wall of the castle only 15 m away, and a small bathing-pier (follow the signs marked *'Portillo'*) only a minute's walk.

～

NEARBY Kastro; Gefyra.
LOCATION within the Kastro of Monemvasia
FOOD self-catering
PRICE €€€
ROOMS 4 double apartments
FACILITIES courtyard bar
CREDIT CARDS MC, V
CHILDREN not suitable
DISABLED not suitable
PETS not accepted
CLOSED never
PROPRIETOR Vasilis Ardamis

LAKONIA

KASTRO, MONEMVASIA

GOULAS

~ VILLAGE GUESTHOUSE ~

23070 Kastro, Monemvasia, Lakonia
TEL 0732 61223 **FAX** 0732 61640

WITH PLENTY OF LOCAL COMPETITION in one of the most sought-after locations in southern Greece, Goulas is undoubtedly among the best places to stay in this unique historic village, only recently discovered by tourism. Housed in the mellow old stone building dating back to the Venetian era are seven rooms, all very comfortably furnished with large double beds, dark wood armoires and whitewashed walls. A sea-facing room is a must – ask for room No. 1 or No. 4, as the other rooms have little or no view. Although the narrow main 'street' of the car-free, fortified village is only a few metres way, Goulas has an extremely quiet location – at night you hear only the sound of the sea. The walled courtyard outside is planted with lemon trees, and there is a small, quiet square a few steps from the front door which looks out to sea.

~

NEARBY Kastro; Gefyra.
LOCATION within old walled village, close to entrance
FOOD breakfast
PRICE €€€€
ROOMS 7; 5 double, 1 triple, 1 double apartment with extra beds; all have shower and WC, phone, TV, minibar
CREDIT CARDS D,V
CHILDREN accepted
DISABLED not suitable
PETS by arrangement
CLOSED never
PROPRIETOR Filio Goulas

LAKONIA

MONEMVASIA

KELLIA INN

~ VILLAGE GUESTHOUSE ~

23070 Kastro, Monemvasia, Lakonia
TEL 0732 61520 **FAX** 0732 6176712

LIKE EVERYTHING ELSE in the Kastro of Monemvasia the Kellia Inn was once something else – in this case, a monks' dormitory. It is still on the ascetic side, with plainly furnished rooms and no luxury embellishments.

Both the guesthouse, and the monastery church, which stands in the broad open space in front of it, are overshadowed by the towering cliffs of Monemvasia. They stand at the edge of the restored part of the ruined Kastro, in a quiet location a little way away from the restaurants and cafés of the narrow main street.

There is plenty of open space, with a big café terrace outside and a courtyard behind. The tourist office runs the inn in an amiably minimalist fashion – it is sometimes hard to find anybody to check you in or out, especially if you arrive mid-afternoon. That said, the Kellia represents excellent value for money in the Kastro, where rooms are often at a premium, and is fine for a short stay. Finding a place to park anywhere near the entrance to the Kastro (which is not accessible to cars) is often a problem. The Kellia is further from the castle entrance than most Kastro hotels, reached by steep and narrow cobbled lanes, and is not recommended for the elderly or families with small children.

~

NEARBY Kastro; Gefyra.
LOCATION within the Kastro of Monemvasia
FOOD breakfast
PRICE €€
ROOMS 11 twin with en suite WC and shower
FACILITIES terrace, courtyard
CREDIT CARDS MC, V
CHILDREN not suitable
DISABLED not suitable
PETS accepted by arrangement
CLOSED never
PROPRIETOR Dimitris Kyriakakis

LAKONIA

MONEMVASIA

HOTEL LAZARETO

~ MANSION HOTEL ~

23070 Kastro, Monemvasia, Lakonia
TEL 0732 61990

THE LAZARETO PROVES THAT looks can be deceptive. At first glance, it seems like a restored old building. In fact, despite its rustic, traditional exterior, designed to meet the stringent rules that govern building in and around Monemvasia's breathtaking ruined fortress, this is a modern hotel. It was built in the late 1990s on the site of an old Turkish prison, close to the yacht and hydrofoil harbour, and set in well-kept gardens, which provide a vivid green contrast to the arid but stunning landscape beyond.

The Lakonia is dramatically overlooked by the towering crag of Monemvasia and faces south-west, across a blue bay to Gefyra village and the mountains of the southern mainland. Its attractive bar-terrace offers a fine place from which to watch the sunset, and although there is no pool there is a stone-built quay with umbrellas, sun-loungers and a bathing ladder just across the road from the hotel. The rooms look over the hotel's oasis-like garden and are well laid out and comfortable with modern furnishings. The surroundings and the fact that it is possible to drive to the door compensate for the fact that the Lazareto is outside the walls of the spectacular fortress, unlike its competitors (see Hotels Malvasia (page 109) and Byzantino (page 115).

~

NEARBY Kastro of Monemvasia; Gefyra.
LOCATION just outside Gefyra village
FOOD breakfast, lunch, dinner
PRICE €€€
ROOMS 14 twin with en suite WC and shower; all rooms have phone, TV, minibar
FACILITIES restaurant, café-bar, garden
CREDIT CARDS MC, V
CHILDREN welcome
DISABLED some ground-floor rooms
PETS accepted
CLOSED never
PROPRIETORS Hotel Lazareto

LAKONIA

MONEMVASIA

HOTEL MALVASIA

∽ MANSION HOTEL ∽

23070 Kastro, Monemvasia, Lakonia
TEL 0732 61323 **FAX** 0732 61722

THIS CHARMING HOTEL was the first in the remarkable medieval walled town of Monemvasia, and is still (but only just) the best although several newer hotels now provide some competition.

The Malvasia must be one of the most atmospheric places to stay in Greece, with large, airy rooms spread over three restored Venetian buildings close to each other in a maze of narrow, car-free lanes. Each of the 14 bedrooms is plainly decorated in individual style, but all have polished wood or flagstone floors, traditional textiles, antique furniture, and fine views south over the Aegean.

The best rooms are in the original Malvasia Hotel, which has a bar-café, where you eat breakfast or enjoy coffee or a drink on a sunny terrace with lovely views. The only fault we could find with the Malvasia is that the service, though friendly, can be a little erratic. There is rarely anybody around at any time other than breakfast. This is the only meal served, but there is a wide choice of restaurants on the main street of Monemvasia, only a few steps away. You can swim from a tiny bathing-pier just outside the walls, less than 100 m from the hotel.

∽

NEARBY Kastro of Monemvasia; beaches.
LOCATION in the centre of a walled medieval town overlooking the Aegean
FOOD breakfast
PRICE €€€
ROOMS 30 twin with WC and shower; all rooms have coffee-making facilities, balcony
FACILITIES café-bar
CREDIT CARDS MC, V
CHILDREN not suitable
DISABLED not suitable
PETS accepted
CLOSED Oct-Apr
PROPRIETOR Ioannis Elias

REPORTING TO THE GUIDE

Please write and tell us about your experiences of small hotels, guest houses and inns, whether good or bad, whether listed in this edition or not. As well as hotels in Greece, we are interested in hotels in France, Spain, Italy, Austria, Germany, Switzerland and the U.S.A. We assume that reporters have no objections to our publishing their views unpaid.

Readers whose reports prove particularly helpful may be invited to join our Travellers' Panel. Members give us notice of their own travel plans; we suggest hotels that they might inspect, and help with the cost of accommodation.

The address is:

Editor, *Charming Small Hotel Guides*,
Duncan Petersen Publishing Limited,
31 Ceylon Road,
London W14 0PY.

Checklist
Please use a separate sheet of paper for each report; include your name, address and telephone number on each report.

Your reports will be received with particular pleasure if they are typed, and if they are organized under the following headings:

Name of establishment
Town or village it is in, or nearest
Full address, including postcode
Telephone number
Time and duration of visit
The building and setting
The public rooms
The bedrooms and bathrooms
Physical comfort (chairs, beds, heat, light, hot water)
Standards of maintenance and housekeeping
Atmosphere, welcome and service
Food
Value for money

We assume that in writing you have no objections to your views being published unpaid, either verbatim or in an edited version. Names of major outside contributors are acknowledged, at the editor's discretion, in the guide.

LAKONIA

PLINTRA

THE ROSE HOUSE
~ FAMILY GUESTHOUSE ~

23052 Plintra, Lakonia
TEL and FAX 0732 82602 **E-MAIL** therosehouse@usa.net

THEY DON'T COME MUCH more cheerfully, cheaply and charmingly out of the way than this very simple blue-and-white painted guesthouse deep in the southern Peloponnese, beside a crescent of sandy beach that, amazingly, remains wholly undiscovered by the holiday industry.

Oleanders and trellised vines shade a simple courtyard surrounding a simple village house, off which are the rooms, in equally simple one-storey cottages, all with whitewashed walls and vivid blue woodwork. Quinces and pomegranates grow in the courtyard and there is a tiny shrine to St Nektarios in the garden. Owner Dimitra Skordallakis has lived in Canada and speaks fluent English, and the place attracts a steady stream of guests who return year after year.

The Rose House is mainly geared up for self-catering (though drinks and snacks are served); there are several *tavernas* in the village nearby. It would be a great place for a family on a budget, with a sandy, toddler-friendly beach just steps away and some music-bar based nightlife in summer for teenagers. The only fly in the ointment is access: getting here by bus is just about possible, but arduous; you really need a car.

~

NEARBY Plintra beach.
LOCATION on beach, 500 m from village
FOOD breakfast, self-catering
PRICE €€
ROOMS 8 double, some family rooms with extra beds
CREDIT CARDS not accepted
CHILDREN welcome
DISABLED not suitable
PETS accepted
CLOSED Nov-Mar
PROPRIETOR Dimitra Skordallakis

ARCADIA

HOTEL MENALON

VILLAGE GUESTHOUSE

22010 Vitina, Arcadia

TEL 0795 22217
FAX 0795 22200
FOOD breakfast
PRICE €€€
CLOSED never
PROPRIETORS Hotel Menalon SA

THE MENALON OCCUPIES its own new building, but pays due attention to the architectural traditions of the region: the exterior features an imaginative and stylish use of decorative brickwork and charming wooden balconies which harmonize well with the older buildings of this sleepy farming village surrounded by the hills of the Arcadian heartland.

Inside is a harmonious blend of traditional and modern, with paintings by contemporary Greek artists contrasting with antiques and textiles from the region. The courtyard is attractive, but it has to be said that service is not always as professionally attentive as you might expect from the general style of the place, and the hotel is often bereft of staff throughout the afternoon. hiking through its spectacular gorges.

TRIKOLONEIO

VILLAGE GUESTHOUSE

22024 Stemnitsa, Arcadia

TEL 0795 81297
FAX 0795 81483
FOOD breakfast
PRICE €€€
CLOSED never
PROPRIETOR Trikoloneio SA

THE TRIKOLONEIO IS A FRIEND-LY, first class guest house which has been created by knocking together two traditional stone-built Arcadian highland mansions into one rambling building around a courtyard overlooking the main street of the village and the village square, next to the church.

The pale stone walls are offset by lots of flowers and greenery, including a pine shaded terrace. Rooms make much use of polished wood and all are en suite. The village is an ideal base for exploring the dramatic scenery of the Lousssios Gorge, and is high in the mountains of Arcadia, where the weather can be pleasantly cooler in summer and downright chilly in winter and early spring – when the big wood fireplace in the lounge is a very welcome sight of an evening.

ARGOLIS

NAFPLION

TAVERNA CHRISTO-PHOROS

TOWN TAVERNA

Staikopoulou 26, 21100 Nafplion

TEL 0752 21131
PRICE €€€
CREDIT CARDS V
CLOSED never

ODOS STAIKOPOULOU, the long, narrow pedestrian street that runs through the pretty old town centre of Nafplion just a few steps from the harbour, is lined with restaurants. This is among the best of the bunch – you can tell, because there are as many Greeks eating here as there are foreign visitors. The *taverna* is prettily decorated inside and out, with mural paintings, blue wooden chairs and tables, and a menu that features all the traditional favourites – fish, chicken, lamb and pork grilled over charcoal, and an assortment of savoury pies and pastries. Christophoros is not about to win any Michelin stars, but for favourite local dishes in friendly, pleasant surroundings it is one of the best bets in town.

LAKONIA

KOTRONAS

KOTRONAS BAY

BEACH HOTEL

23066 Kotronas, Lakonia

TEL 0733 21340
FAX 0733 21400
E-MAIL kotoronas@otenet.gr

THE KOTRONAS BAY is new, immaculately designed, located and run. Owner Mary Panagakos is a well-known Greek TV chef, and her *taverna*, adjoining the bungalows, serves traditional Greek dishes made from fresh local ingredients, local olive oil and wine from the barrel. The bungalows are set in terraced gardens and all have beautiful east-facing views of a calm blue bay.

A rocky path leads down to a tiny, virtually private sheltered beach (a mixture of pebbles, shingle and sand) with very clear water. Above this is a terrace with white plastic sun loungers beneath the shade of olive trees and pink flowering oleanders. Each room is prettily decorated in village style and is equipped with two built in sofas that can become single beds, as well as a properly equipped kitchen.

LAKONIA

LIMENI

LIMENI VILLAGE HOTEL

RESORT HOTEL

23062 Limeni, Lakonia

TEL 0733 51111
FAX 0733 51182
FOOD breakfast, lunch, dinner
PRICE €€€€
CLOSED never
PROPRIETORS Tourist Enterprises
N. Petroulas SA

THE LIMENI VILLAGE is a successful compromise between the unique vernacular architecture of the Mani and the comforts of a modern resort-style hotel, including what is indisputably the best swimming pool in the Mani region (admittedly from a choice of only three hotels with pools). There are fabulous views, too, over Itilo bay, surrounded by steep hillsides, to the grim grey slopes of the Pentadaktilos mountains and the ruined ramparts of Kelefa castle. The rooms are built in sensitive imitation of Mani tower houses, and spread down the hillside, with most rooms clustered around the pool and its stone-walled terrace; creepers and maturing palm trees and shrubs soften the outlines of the stonework. The rooms have stone floors, rugs, and wooden bed platforms and are simply decorated.

MONEMVASIA

TO KANONI

VILLAGE RESTAURANT

23070 Kastro, Monemvasia

TEL 0732 61387
PRICE €€€
CREDIT CARDS V
CLOSED Nov-Easter

To Kanoni (named after the muzzle-loading Venetian cannon which sits on the church square outside) is Monemvasia's best restaurant, with an unpretentious menu listing all the Greek favourites; the fish is particularly good. It can get very crowded in summer and at weekends, when the Kastro attracts hordes of Athenians, but non-Greeks (who usually prefer to eat earlier in the evening) should have no problem finding a table. To Kanoni has four terraces, including two roof terraces and two at street level, as well as tables indoors. For the best view, sit on the roof. Alternatively, there are tables on the street, too, mainly patronized by those just having a snack or a drink.

LAKONIA

MIKINES

HOTEL BELLE HELENE

VILLAGE GUESTHOUSE

21200 Mikines

TEL 0751 76225
FAX 0751 76179
FOOD breakfast, lunch, dinner
PRICE €
CLOSED never
PROPRIETORS Hotel Belle Helene

M OST VISITORS TO THE wonderfully evocative ancient ruins of Mycenae come by coach or car, spend a few hours at most, then vanish. A far better way to savour the atmosphere is to stay in this simple guesthouse in a 19th neoclassical building. Schliemann, the archaeologist who rediscovered ancient Mycenae in the late 19th century, stayed here, the guest book reveals, as did a number of other well-known names. On the main street of Mikines village, the Hotel Belle Helene has large, simply furnished rooms, and provides comfortable, peaceful lodgings, making it an ideal place to spend one or two nights while touring the antiquities of the Peloponnese.

MONEMVASIA

HOTEL BYZANTINO

TOWN HOUSE HOTEL

23070 Kastro, Monemvasia, Lakonia

TEL 0732 61254
FOOD breakfast, lunch, dinner, snacks
PRICE €€€
CLOSED never
PROPRIETOR Ioannis Traiforos

L IKE ITS RIVAL, THE MALVASIA, the Byzantino is a collection of individual houses scattered around the narrow, pedestrian-only lanes of the ruined Kastro. Its reception, bar and restaurant are on the main street, opposite the church square, and some of the rooms are in the same building and can be noisy in high season. The Byzantino is friendly, with plenty of character, and some of the rooms are charming, with flagstone floors, vaulted ceilings and plain whitewashed walls. Quality control, however, is spotty; the last time we stayed here, in a recently restored ground-floor room, there was an infestation of woodlice in the shower room, which seemed to surprise none of the staff.

HOTEL BYZANTION

VILLAGE HOTEL

23100 Mystras, Sparti

TEL 0731 83309
FAX 0731 20019
FOOD breakfast, lunch, dinner;
room service
PRICE €€€
CLOSED never
PROPRIETORS Medotels
International

THE BYZANTION HAS an unfair advantage: it is not just the best hotel in Mistras, but the only hotel in Mistras. Built in 1964 and last renovated in 1998, it has an arcaded design reminiscent of classical architecture. However, it earns its entry here on the strength of its location, in the centre of a quiet village and a short distance from the remarkable ruined Byzantine city of Mistras. The colour scheme and furniture in the lobby and bedrooms are best described as inoffensive, but the service is brisk and professional, geared mainly towards the escorted tour groups which occasionally stop off here. Your stay will be memorable more for the sight of the fairytale ruined palaces of the Byzantine despots than for the hotel.

IONIAN ISLANDS

The Ionian islands include (from north to south) Corfu, Paxos, Levkas, Kefalonia, Ithaki, Zakinthos and (the joker in the pack, far off to the south east between Cape Tainaron and Crete), Kithira. They share a common history as possessions (from the 13th to late 18th century) of Venice and (briefly, in the first half of the 19th century) of Britain. More recently, they have been subject to a second British colonization, this time by the package tourist industry and its clients. Corfu and Zakinthos between them receive almost one million British holidaymakers each summer, and Levkas and Kefalonia are increasingly popular.

As a result, most of the accommodation on these islands is geared to the needs of mass-market tour operators and their clients and meets none of the requirements of this book. However, we have found a surprising number of charming places to stay in Corfu, while remote Kithira proved an unexpectedly rich lode, with more than its fair share of attractive little hotels and guesthouses.

Kithira excepted, the Ionian islands are generally greener and a little cooler than those of the Aegean. Their architecture has been strongly influenced by their centuries under Venetian rule and most of the hotels we list in Corfu are in genteel Italianate buildings. Kithira is again the exception, with dazzling whitewashed village houses that would not look out of place in the Cyclades, and its own distinctive vernacular architecture.

Tourism in all the Ionian islands is highly seasonal, with charter flights to Corfu, Kefalonia, Zakinthos and Preveza (for Levkas) from April to October, and domestic scheduled flights, via Athens to all of these and Kithira, year round. Very few places stay open all year round, and most are closed between October and Easter. Summer temperatures, while still reliably sunny, are marginally cooler than elsewhere in Greece, and spring and autumn rain is also more likely than in other islands and mainland regions.

CORFU

HOTEL MARINDA
~ VILLAGE HOTEL ~

49100 Agios Ioannis, Triklino, Corfu
TEL and **FAX** 0661 52410

THIS OLD-FASHIONED, Corfiot-Italianate inn on a quiet street in the centre of one of Corfu's less visited villages will appeal to those who like their grandeur slightly faded. Arches on the ground floor support an upper storey with whitewashed stone walls and green-painted window shutters, and there is a pretty garden filled with greenery at the back of the building, where tall palm trees shade a paved patio. Opening on to the garden is a small bar and breakfast room.

The cool, high ceilinged lobby is paved in pink and white marble, and the walls are hung with prints of Corfiots in traditional island costume. A wooden stairway leads up to an upper floor of high, airy rooms with tall windows and simple furniture. Off the lobby on the ground floor is a sitting room furnished with antique armchairs, old prints and paintings of Corfu, a grand piano, antique chests and some pretty inlaid Italian tables.

All in all, the Marinda is a pretty exercise in nostalgia, and will appeal to visitors who arrive in Corfu with hopes of finding the world (sadly vanished) that Gerald Durrell wrote about in his memoir of the island in the 1930s, *My Family and Other Animals*. Quiet though it is, Agios Ioannis is only minutes from west coast beaches, and only 15 minutes' drive from Corfu town.

~

NEARBY beaches; Corfu town.
LOCATION 12 km west of Corfu town, 3 km from west coast
FOOD breakfast
PRICE €€€
ROOMS 10, all double or twin with shower and WC
FACILITIES bar, sitting room, garden
CREDIT CARDS V
CHILDREN accepted
DISABLED not suitable **PETS** by arrangement
CLOSED Oct-Mar
PROPRIETOR Vasilos Koskinas-Rombolitis

CORFU

HOTEL BELLA VENEZIA
~ TOWN HOTEL ~

4 N. Zambeli, 49100 Corfu
TEL 0661 46500 **Fax** 0661 20708
E-MAIL belvenht@hol.gr

This recently renovated neoclassical building stands on a quiet street a short distance from the Spianada, Corfu town's pretty central park. The exterior is elegant, with immaculate stucco work and a rather grand entrance portico which supports a balustraded balcony. Inside, the lobby has soft lighting and polished marble floors; the sitting room and bar have carved wooden ceilings.

The rooms are smallish, with very high ceilings (typical of the period during which the hotel was built) and shuttered windows which reach almost from floor to ceiling. Some have canopied four-poster beds. They are cool and comfortable enough, but are not rooms in which you would choose to spend much time except when resting. Fortunately, the hotel has a spacious and sunny garden, full of flowers and shrubs, where you can eat breakfast, or sit.

The Bella Venezia does not have its own swimming pool, but it does have an arrangement for its guests to use the smart Corfu Nautical Club, which has a private beach and water sports only 100 m away from the hotel. The restaurants, shops and museums of one of Greece's prettiest island towns are all within walking distance.

~

NEARBY historic town centre; castle; harbour; airport.
LOCATION town centre
FOOD breakfast, lunch, dinner
PRICE €€€
ROOMS 32 all with shower and WC; all rooms have phone, TV, central heating, air conditioning
FACILITIES bar, restaurant, garden
CREDIT CARDS MC, V
CHILDREN accepted
DISABLED not suitable **PETS** by arrangement
CLOSED never
PROPRIETOR Theodoros Ziniatis

CORFU

HOTEL CAVALIERI

～ TOWN HOTEL ～

4 Capodistriou, 49100 Corfu
TEL 0661 39041 **FAX** 0661 39283
E-MAIL info@cavalieri-hotel.com

FIRST IMPRESSIONS OF the Cavalieri are of faded grandeur, but in fact there is nothing faded about this grand old hotel. The Cavalieri was created in 1967, behind the façade of a 17thC mansion which originally belonged to one of Corfu's Venetian noble families, the Flamburiari. The hotel has recently been completely renovated, with the addition of a lovely roof terrace which has stunning views of the old town and the castle and is the perfect place for an evening drink.

Public areas are thoughtfully decorated, with contrasting black and white marble tiles in the lobby and sitting room, antique mirrors, parquet-floored dining room, flowery wallpaper in pastel shades, and chairs and sofas upholstered in cream and raspberry pink. Bedrooms are comfortably furnished with Venetian-period antiques or more modern reproduction furniture and wall to wall carpets; curtains and other soft furnishings are in bright English chintzes. Virtually all the rooms have fine views, and in terms of location in Corfu town the Cavalieri is unbeatable, beside the Spianada and with all the attractions of Corfu town on the doorstep.

～

NEARBY harbour; airport, castle; museums; historic town centre.
LOCATION town centre
FOOD breakfast, lunch, dinner
PRICE €€€€
ROOMS 45 double and single, and maisonette suites with bathroom; all roms have phone, TV, air conditioning, minibar, internet connection
FACILITIES restaurant, bar, TV, card room
CREDIT CARDS MC, V
CHILDREN accepted
DISABLED not suitable
PETS by arrangement
CLOSED never
PROPRIETORS Cavalieri Hotel SA

CORFU

FUNDANA VILLAS

~ COUNTRY HOTEL ~

PO Box 167, 49100 Skripero Corfu
TEL 0663 22532 **FAX** 0663 22453

THIS SUPERB, HACIENDA-LIKE hideaway among pine and olive trees is at the end of a very rough track, perched on a hill overlooking wide open farmland, pastures and pine woods, and with serious mountain slopes on the further horizon. The red-painted, pantiled bungalows were purpose-built in 1988 and surround a lovely old Venetian mansion, dating from the 17th century and with mellow distressed paint and plaster that would be the envy of many a designer.

Each bungalow has a sitting/dining room, double bedroom and two divan beds, as well as its own share of a gravel patio area with white plastic sun loungers. There are more of these by the pool, which is on a terrace under the shade of orange, almond and olive trees and the evenings are scented by the flowers of citrus and jasmine.

The reception area was once an olive press and is a cool, dark vaulted space with a bar in a corner, cobbled floor, heavy dark wood beams supporting the roof and three café tables. The massive old wooden oil press and stone grinding wheels are still in place, and a small stone well in the garden outside is still in use. This is mainly a spot for those who like the flexibility of self-catering, as service is limited to twice-weekly cleaning and linen change, though breakfast can be served on request.

NEARBY Paleokastritsa beach; Corfu town; harbour, airport.
LOCATION hillside 1.4 km west of main road, 3 km south of Paleokastritsa beach
FOOD breakfast, self catering
PRICE €€€€
ROOMS 7 bungalows sleeping four, all with WC and shower, kitchen, private patio
FACILITIES pool, gardens, restaurant, bar, video room, swimming pool
CREDIT CARDS not accepted
CHILDREN welcome
DISABLED access difficult **PETS** welcome
CLOSED Nov-Mar
PROPRIETOR Spyros Spathas

CORFU

SGOMBOU

CASA LUCIA
~ COUNTRY HOTEL ~

49083 Sgombou, Corfu
TEL 0661 91419 **FAX** 0661 91732

CASA LUCIA IS a collection of colourful cottages in a lush garden with immaculate lawns, palm trees, bougainvillea and flowers. Val and Dennis Anagnostopoulos bought the old olive press, house and stables here in 1977 and Dennis, an interior designer, restored the building with its thick stone walls, beams, and stone arches. Each cottage is colourfully and individually decorated, with colourful cotton rugs, striped woollen blankets or patchwork quilts on beds and sofas. Some have separate living rooms with an additional sofa bed, others have beds on mezzanine platforms. Colours are gentle shades of cream, blue and pink exteriors with whitewashed walls and dark woodwork inside. Each cottage has its own private patio area. Bed linen is changed twice weekly and rooms are cleaned and towels replaced six times per week.

The gardens are very large and there is a large, oval swimming pool, shaded by trees and with a shallow end for children and plenty of sun beds and lounging chairs. Casa Lucia is a perfect, quiet family holiday spot: it is hard to believe that the raucous nightlife and mass-market resorts of the Corfu coast are only a few minutes' drive away.

~

NEARBY beaches at Ipsos, Dassia, Paleokastritsa; historic Corfu town; port; airport; Mt Pantokrato.r
LOCATION Sgombou, 12 km west of Corfu town on Paleokastritsa road
FOOD snacks, self-catering
PRICE €€€ - €€€€
ROOMS 6 cottages sleeping 2-4; 2 studios sleeping 1-2; 2 cottages sleeping 4-5, all with shower and WC, kitchen
FACILITIES gardens, pool
CREDIT CARDS not accepted
CHILDREN welcome
DISABLED limited access to 2 cottages **PETS** by arrangement
CLOSED Oct-Apr 1
PROPRIETORS Val and Dennis Anagnostopoulos

KEFALONIA

FISKARDO

ERISOS

~ VILLAGE GUESTHOUSE ~

28084 Fiskardo, Kefalonia
TEL 0674 41327

Just two steps from Fiskardo's pretty harbour (very popular with yachts), Erisos is a spic-and-span little guesthouse in a 190-year-old, two-storey village house, in tidy pale yellow coloured paint. It is in sharp contrast with the old building next door, which is picturesquely dilapidated, with faded, distressed plaster and paint.

Geraniums in pots grow outside the front door and a colossal bougainvillea vine grows all the way up to the roof. Located on the corner of a narrow lane and a small, quiet village square, Erisos does not have much in the way of a view but in such a pretty village this hardly seems to matter.

The ground-floor reception area (originally the house's living-room-kitchen) has a stone floor and pine plank ceiling, and a wooden staircase leads up to the bedrooms on the floor above, which are simple with tiled floors, whitewashed walls, tall shuttered windows and pine beds. A shared fridge and basic kitchen facilities are also available downstairs, and one of the rooms has a large balcony which overhangs the lane outside. Service is minimal, and this is very much a place for people who want to cater for themselves, though with plenty of pleasant restaurants and cafés nearby, cooking is far from essential.

~

NEARBY harbour; small beach.
LOCATION village centre
FOOD self-catering
PRICE €€
ROOMS 4 twin; 2 with shower and WC, 2 sharing shower and WC
FACILITIES kitchen, breakfast room
CREDIT CARDS not accepted
CHILDREN not suitable
DISABLED not suitable
PETS by arrangement
CLOSED Oct-Apr
PROPRIETOR Spyridoula Manousaridou

KITHIRA

ARONIADIKA

KAMARES

⁓ VILLAGE GUESTHOUSE ⁓

80100 Aroniadika, Kithira
TEL and **FAX** 0735 33420

KAMARES LOOKS RATHER GRAND: a big, whitewashed village house, built a century ago by one of Aroniadika's more prosperous citizens and turned into a guesthouse in 1987. Each apartment has its own blue-painted front door, beneath a wooden pergola and opening on to a raised courtyard where flowers and shrubs flourish in old terracotta oil jars. You look out over the surrounding fields and farmland (rooms 5 to 8 have the best views), with a glimpse of the sea between Kithira and the southern mainland. Each apartment has a fully equipped kitchen, and although rooms are regularly serviced, this is a house intended for self-catering guests – don't expect such frills as room service or ever-present staff.

Aroniadika is primarily a farming village, and tumbledown dry-stone walls and old farm buildings surround the house. It is a great place in which to experience real Greek village life (the main *taverna* is only five minutes' walk away). The village is in the centre of the island, with beaches, Byzantine and Venetian castles and both the ferry ports within a 15 km radius, but there is practically no local transport and you will need a rented car.

There's parking right outside the house.

⁓

NEARBY Aroniadika village; airport; Venetian castle at Palaiochora; Osios Theodoros monastery.
LOCATION village outskirts
FOOD self-catering
PRICE €€€
ROOMS 5 twin-bedded apartments, each with own front door, en suite shower and WC, fully equipped kitchen
FACILITIES courtyard
CREDIT CARDS not accepted
CHILDREN welcome
DISABLED not suitable **PETS** welcome
CLOSED Nov-Mar
PROPRIETOR Panagiotis Mavromatis

KITHIRA

CHORA

HOTEL MARGARITA

∼ ISLAND HOTEL ∼

80100 Chora, Kithira
TEL 0735 31711 **FAX** 0735 31325

THE MARGARITA STANDS just off the main street – really a lane – of Chora, the dazzlingly pretty historic capital of one of Greece's least spoiled islands. It's a dignified, two-storey mansion, built in 1840 by one of the island's leading families and turned into a boutique hotel in 1990 by Linda and Panayotis Fatseas.

The hotel perches above a steep valley, its slopes covered with terraced fields, and has fantastic sunset views from its two terraces, and from most of the rooms. Outside are two stone-paved courtyards, where breakfast is served at blue-painted wooden tables with chequered tablecloths, under white canvas umbrellas.

Most of the rooms are spacious, with some charming period features such as stone arches and stone-tiled floors, and are neutrally and unfussily decorated and furnished with simple wooden beds, chairs and side tables. The Margarita is very much a family-run place, with friendly and professional service. There are several eating places in the village, and more at Kapsali, the miniature harbour 1.5 km below Chora, where you can swim and sunbathe. You could stay here for up to a week; more than that, and you might start wishing for a pool or a handier beach location.

∼

NEARBY Venetian castle; Kapsali harbour and beach.
LOCATION in Chora village
FOOD breakfast, snacks
PRICE €€€
ROOMS 12, all with en suite WC and shower, TV, phone, air conditioning
FACILITIES sitting room, two terraces
CREDIT CARDS V
CHILDREN accepted
DISABLED not suitable
PETS by arrangement
Closed never
PROPRIETORS Panayotis and Linda Fatseas

KITHIRA

KAPSALI

HOTEL RAIKOS

∽ ISLAND HOTEL ∽

80100 Kapsali, Kithira
TEL 0735 31629 **FAX** 0735 31801

THE ONLY CRITICISM we could make of the Raikos is that it is perhaps a little unreal – a shade too much like a holiday brochure hotel, built in imitation of an island village, with dazzling white walls, blue woodwork and bunches of crimson bougainvillea.

It has the only swimming pool in this part of the island (just as well, since the beach is a steep hike away) and is one of the very few places to stay on Kithira which offers something approximating to full-service accommodation, though without such frills as round the clock room service.

Its surroundings are unbeatable, with views of the surrounding terraced hills and olive groves, out to sea over the pretty, tiny port of Kapsali (where you can swim in brilliantly clear water), and uphill to the crumbling battlements of a 16thC Venetian castle. Raikos is a 'village within a village', with its low-rise blocks of rooms connected by stone paved paths. On our last visit (to be fair, at the very end of the summer holiday season) the garden terraces were a little unkempt.

Rooms are modern in style, neutrally decorated and unfussy, and if they lack some of the character of the bedrooms in older island guesthouses on Kithira, they compensate with modern comfort and great views. For a longer stay of one or two weeks on Kithira, the Raikos is certainly your best bet..

∽

NEARBY Kapsali harbour and beach; Chora village; Venetian castle.
LOCATION hillside 750 m above Kapsali harbour and 1 km below Chora
Food breakfast, lunch, dinner
PRICE €€€
ROOMS 25 double or twin, all with en suite shower, WC, phone, TV
Facilities restaurant, bar, swimming pool
CREDIT CARDS DC, MC, V
CHILDREN welcome
DISABLED not suitable **PETS** welcome
CLOSED Oct-Apr
PROPRIETORS Hotel Raikos SA

KITHIRA

PITSINADES

PITSINADES

~ VILLAGE GUESTHOUSE ~

80100 Pitsinades, Aroniadika, Kithira
TEL and **FAX** 0735 33420

THIS STURDY, TWO-STOREY HOUSE with its red-tiled roof and whitewashed walls is a landmark on the outskirts of a picturesquely tumbledown, part-deserted village. The house – which is more than 170 years old – is a fine example of island architecture, with exposed stone window surrounds, arched doorways and lavender-blue paintwork. It has been carefully restored.

Beside the house, within high whitewashed walls, are two pretty court-yards with pebble mosaics, blue and pink painted outbuildings, potted geraniums and small palm trees, and a shady vine arbour. From these, as from the upstairs bedroom windows, there are great views over the surrounding countryside. Staying here is like staying in a family home, and it will suit those looking for pretty surroundings, rather than a service hotel in a holiday resort. You will need a car to get to the beach and to explore the island.

~

NEARBY Aroniadika village; airport; Venetian castle at Palaiochora; Osios Theodoros monastery.
LOCATION Pitsinades village
FOOD breakfast, self-catering
PRICE €€€
ROOMS 4 double, all with en suite shower and WC; 1 3-bed apartment with en suite shower, WC and kitchen.
FACILITIES courtyard
CREDIT CARDS not accepted
CHILDREN welcome
DISABLED not suitable
PETS welcome
CLOSED Nov-Mar
PROPRIETOR Eleni Giannikaki

KITHIRA

TA SFENDONIA
~ VILLAGE GUESTHOUSE ~

80100 Pitsinades, Aroniadika
TEL 0735 33570 **FAX** 01 9513920

A HIGH STONE wall surrounds this tall, whitewashed house in a tumble-down, partly deserted village only a couple of kilometres from Aroniadika. A feature of the garden is the free-standing old stone arch, all that remains of an older building. These arches ('*sfendonia*') are a typical feature of Kithiran island architecture, and give the house its name. An arched gateway leads through the outer wall into a flower-filled courtyard dominated by two more huge arches which support the upper storey of the house and make a pleasant, shady place to sit; or you can mellow out beneath a pretty fresco of two white doves of peace. Walnut trees and clumps of jasmine shade the rear garden and the courtyard.

Sfendonia has a long pedigree. Built in the 17th century, it was origi-nally the home of the village priest (there is a small church nearby). Many of the house's original features have been preserved or restored, including mosaic floors and carved ceilings, and the sitting rooms are furnished with old stone beehives, grindstones and the family olive press.

From the upstairs bedroom windows there are fine views over the windswept uplands and farmland of Kithira. Ta Sfendonia, like most places to stay on Kithira, is intended for people who want a self-catering holiday, and there are cafés and *tavernas* at Aroniadika, within walking distance.

NEARBY Aroniadika village; airport; Venetian castle at Palaiochora; Osios Theodoros monastery.
LOCATION Pitsinades village
FOOD breakfast, self-catering
PRICE ©©©
ROOMS 3 double-bedded apartments, all with extra bed, en suite shower and WC, kitchenette
FACILITIES shared sitting room, courtyard
CREDIT CARDS not accepted **CHILDREN** welcome **DISABLED** not suitable
PETS by arrangement **CLOSED** Oct-Mar
PROPRIETOR Anna Tsihli

KITHIRA

POTAMOS

PORFYRA
~ VILLAGE GUESTHOUSE ~

80200 Potamos, Kithira
TEL 0735 33329

ONE OF THE very few places to stay on Kithira which remains open all year round, Porfyra is on the main street of the island's largest village and is named after the shellfish which abound in the nearby waters and which were prized by the Romans and Byzantines for the purple dye they produced. A blue-painted door leads from the street into a paved courtyard with blindingly white walls which contrast with bright blue wooden shutters and doors. Above the courtyard are shady balconies, and at ground level there are white canvas sun umbrellas, loungers and chairs.

Rooms are simply furnished, and rather more lavishly equipped than most on the island, and have luxuries such as televisions. With a selection of cafés and *tavernas* on the main square of the village, just a few metres away, Porfyra is a great place for those who want to experience life in a typical island village which (except in July and August when hundreds of Greek-Australians flock back to their ancestral island) seems to have been little affected by tourism. Bedrooms are regularly cleaned and serviced, but Porfyra is not a full-service hotel.

~

NEARBY village; airport; Venetian castle at Palaiochora; Osios Theodoros monastery.
LOCATION centre of Potamos village
FOOD breakfast
PRICE €€€
ROOMS 7, all with double and single bed, en suite shower and WC, phone, TV, central heating, refrigerator
FACILITIES courtyard
CREDIT CARDS not accepted
CHILDREN welcome
DISABLED access difficult
PETS welcome
CLOSED never
PROPRIETOR Anastasia Megalokonomou

CORFU

CORFU PALACE HOTEL

TOWN HOTEL

Leoforos Democratias 2, 49100 Corfu

TEL 0661 39485 FAX 0661 31749
E-MAIL cfupalace@hol.gr
PRICE €€
CREDIT CARDS AE, MC, V
CLOSED never
PROPRIETORS Hotel Corfu Palace SA

THIS TRULY PALATIAL hotel will appeal to those looking for resort hotel comfort and facilities, yet within walking distance of the pretty, historic old town of Corfu and away from the excesses of the island's less exclusive, mass market holiday resort areas. It is a long, cream-coloured building on the esplanade which runs along the waterfront, with a fine view of the bustling harbour and the mainland hills opposite. Inside, the lobby is grand, but somewhat bland, and this is also true of the rooms. That said, the level of comfort, excellent service and luxury facilities more than compensate, and the hotel is also one of a handful of properties in Corfu which stay open year round.

PELECAS COUNTRY CLUB

COUNTRY HOTEL

Pelecas, 49100 Corfu
TEL 0661 52239 FAX 0661 52919
PRICE €€€€
CREDIT CARDS not accepted
CLOSED never
PROPRIETOR Nikos Velianitis

THE PELECAS COUNTRY Club is tucked away in the hills roughly midway between Corfu town and Paleokastritsa and seems determined to maintain its reputation for upmarket exclusivity by being hard to find. Owner Nikos Velianitis has lovingly converted his family's 18thC mansion and the surrounding estate buildings (formerly stables, olive presses or wine cellars) into a complex of luxury living quarters, all furnished with finely restored antiques (some of them dating from the era of the 19thC British protectorate, some from Florence). One apartment even has the armchair of King George II of the Hellenes. Staying here is very much like having a private villa, but with a communal bar, swimming pool and tennis courts.

CORFU

REX

TOWN RESTAURANT

66 Capodistriou, 49100 Corfu

TEL 0661 39649
PRICE €€
CREDIT CARDS V
CLOSED never

A CORFU INSTITUTION since 1932, the Rex has been rated among the top ten restaurants in Greece and is very popular with local people – always a good sign. It is in a 19thC house, with tables spilling out on to the street, and serves all the usual Greek favourites from rabbit in wine sauce to chicken in lemon, local specialities such as *sofrito* and *pastitsada*, and heartier dishes such as *moussaka* and *giouvetsi*. There are also some exotic dishes such as chicken in kumquat sauce and peppery swordfish *bourdetto*. The smartly dressed waiters are friendly and brisk, and the wine list is much broader than in run-of-the-mill tourist restaurants, with wines from all over Greece.

KEFALONIA

RESTAURANT TASSIA

VILLAGE RESTAURANT

28084 Fiskardo, Kefalonia

TEL 0674 41205
PRICE €€
CREDIT CARDS V
CLOSED Oct-Mar

T ASSIA DENDRINOU-KATOPODI'S quayside restaurant in Fiskardo has won praise from dozens of Greek and international critics whose articles are given pride of place on the walls. There is no better location in Fiskardo, right on the harbour, and the menu is imaginative, with fish soup, fresh lobster, lamb, mussels, pasta dishes, charcoal-grilled meat and fish and traditional Kefalonia meat and rice pie all clamouring for attention.

Outside, tables and chairs are painted lavender blue, and stand on a car-free quayside. Inside, the restaurant is beautifully and colourfully decorated, with cushioned wall benches; the ceiling is panelled wood in red, cream and turquoise. The wine list is extensive, and the service attentive. You will want to eat here more than once.

KITHIRA

ROUGA

TRADITIONAL GUESTHOUSE

80100 Aroniadika, Kithira

TEL AND FAX 0735 33596
FOOD self-catering
PRICE €€
CLOSED never
PROPRIETORS Susan and Panagiotis Magonesos

Susy and Panagiotis have been running this attractive, two-century-old building on the quiet outskirts of Aroniadika village since 1990. The house is prettily whitewashed, and draped in ivy and bougainvillea.

Upstairs, a little terrace is shared between pairs of rooms, with attractive views over the high, windswept plateau of Kithira island and the rooftops of the village. Aroniadika is very definitely for those in search of peace and quiet, with no nightlife and only a couple of very simple *tavernas* in the village. There are beaches not too far away, but none within walking distance, so a car will really be an essential when staying here.

NORTHERN AEGEAN

IN ANCIENT TIMES, the islands of the Aegean were divided into the 'Cyclades' or 'encircling' islands (those which surrounded the sacred isle of Delos) and the 'Sporades' or 'scattered' islands, comprising all the rest. For the purposes of this book, the Northern Aegean islands include those in the group now known as the Sporades – four small islands and one large one, all quite close to the northern mainland – as well as those now classified for administrative puroposes as the North-east Aegean islands.

Not all of these have charming small hotels worthy of inclusion in this book (though that may soon change, and we look forward to readers' recommendations), but we have located some very attractive places to stay on Skiathos and Skopelos in the Sporades as well as one outstanding property on neighbouring Evia (Greece's second largest island) and some charming village guesthouses on Chios, an island so far completely undiscovered by mass tourism.

The Sporades (and especially Skiathos,which has an international airport with charter flights in summer, and some magnificent sandy beaches) have become popular package holiday islands, but development has not been allowed to run riot. It has to be said that the main reason for coming here is for a sun and sand family holiday, and with that in mind we have included a couple of medium-sized, resort-style hotels which meet the needs of sunseekers but which also have a certain amount of personality. Location, too, has played a major part in the selection process. Skopelos is a very different island, sees fewer visitors and has pebbly rather than sandy beaches, and we list two charming small hotels in its pretty harbour village, a few steps from the waterfront.

Elsewhere in the region, Chios – a large island within sight of the Turkish coast and a character all of its own – has a rich and unique village architecture, and only lack of space hinders us from including a number of traditional properties on this charming island.

Like Greece's southern and Ionian islands, those of the Northern Aegean are for visiting in spring, summer and autumn,with little to offer in winter, and most hotels close from October or November to April. This is not really a region for island-hopping – the North-east Aegean islands are far apart – though Skiathos and Skopelos are close together and connected by fast and frequent hydrofoils. Getting to the North-east Aegean islands can also be a bit of a challenge, requiring a change of plane in Athens (or, if you prefer to go by sea, an overnight ferry crossing from the mainland port of Rafina, close to Athens International Airport).

SPORADES

CHORA, SKOPELOS

HOTEL ARCHONTIKO

~ VILLAGE HOTEL ~

37003 Chora, Skopelos
TEL *0424 22765*

THIS STURDY WHITE BUILDING with its black gloss shutters, balconies and window frames is set a little way back from the waterfront in Chora's maze of apparently nameless streets and lanes – difficult to find. It is worth phoning ahead and advising them which boat you will arrive on, so that a guide can meet you at the pier. Originally the home of one of the island's more prosperous citizens, it was built in 1880 and converted into an inn in 1981 by the present owner.

The rooms are spacious, light and airy, but without a view of the harbour, and only one has its own bathroom; the rest share one bathroom for every two rooms. The hotel has two small courtyards under vine trellises, as well as a breakfast room and a couple of trestle tables on the street outside where you can sit and watch the world go by. Service is friendly and attentive at breakfast time, but largely conspicuous by its absence for the rest of the day, and this is not a hotel for those who require round the clock room service or full scale hotel facilities. Nor is it, perhaps, ideal for a longer stay, but it is a very pleasant spot for a few days on an island-hopping tour around the Sporades.

~

NEARBY village shops and restaurants; ferry harbour.
LOCATION in centre of village
FOOD breakfast
PRICE €€€
ROOMS 9; 7 double, 2 triple, 1 with en-suite WC and shower; all rooms have phone
FACILITIES breakfast room, courtyard
CREDIT CARDS not accepted
CHILDREN accepted
DISABLED not suitable
PETS accepted by arrangement
CLOSED never
PROPRIETOR Angeliki Kotsoridou

SPORADES

CHORA, SKOPELOS

PENSION KIR SOTOS

~ VILLAGE HOTEL ~

37003 Chora, Skopelos
TEL 0424 22549 **FAX** 0424 23668

THIS CHARMING, HIGGLEDY-PIGGLEDY little pension is right on the broad, tree-lined quayside of Skopelos's pretty main village. The building is more than 120 years old, and was converted into a hotel in 1983. All the rooms are slightly different in shape and size, but all are plainly furnished, with varnished pine floors and ceilings and whitewashed walls. Most windows overlook the bay and the port where ferries and hydrofoils dock – only a minute's walk away, making Kir Sotos one of the most convenient places to stay on Skopelos. There is a small paved courtyard, surrounded by high stone walls, and a roof terrace where you can sit, eat and drink.

Service is minimal, and limited to room cleaning, dishwashing and reception (not staffed round the clock). The idea is that you prepare your own breakfast, without the drudgery of washing up afterwards. There is a basic kitchen with cooking rings, a refrigerator and a dishwasher. In this respect, Kir Sotos feels more like your own rented home than a typical pension, and it is also extremely good value for money. The only possible snag is that there are no beaches within easy walking distance, so it is not ideal for families with smaller children. To balance that, the many restaurants and cafés of this attractive, old-fashioned island village are right on your doorstep.

~

NEARBY harbour; village shops and restaurants.
LOCATION on waterfront in main island village
FOOD limited self-catering
PRICE €€
ROOMS 12 double and twin with en suite WC and shower
FACILITIES kitchen, courtyard
CREDIT CARDS V
CHILDREN accepted
DISABLED not suitable **PETS** not accepted
CLOSED Nov-Mar
PROPRIETOR Alexandra Dimitriadis

SPORADES

CANDILI
~ FAMILY ESTATE ~

Achmetage, Prokopi, Evia
TEL 00 44 1580 766 599 **FAX** 00 44 1580 765 416
E-MAIL holidays@elysianholidays.co.uk

THE MANOR HOUSE AND ESTATE at Achmetaga, set among fields, olive groves and wooded hills in northern Evia, have been in the hands of the Noel-Baker family since the 19th century. They have now been transformed into a unique place to stay, with a choice of accommodation which includes rooms in Konaki, the family house, or in the Candili wing, converted from the estate's granary. Each of these has its own garden and plunge pool and a recent and very welcome addition is a 15-m swimming pool which can be used by all guests on the estate.

The family cook prepares excellent authentic Greek dishes from locally grown produce, which are served at a communal table, and there is thrice-weekly maid service. Ideal for couples is the self-catering, self-contained Ktounia cottage, with its own plunge pool (but without electricity or other modern conveniences), about 20 minutes' walk from the main buildings. Candili also has a seaside summer house, 90 minutes' drive from the estate on a peninsula of more than one hectare, gloriously isolated and perfect for those who prefer to be on the coast. Candili also offers a wide selection of creative summer courses, including painting and pottery.

~

NEARBY beaches at Rovies; Galataki monastery.
LOCATION Prokopi, 52 km N of Halkida
FOOD lunch, dinner
PRICE €€€€
ROOMS 12 double in Candili wing; 5 twin or double (1 with en suite bathroom) in Konaki; double with en suite bath and 2 sofa beds in Ktounia cottage; double in Limniona cottage
FACILITIES sitting room, dining room, study, library, garden, swimming pool
CREDIT CARDS not accepted
CHILDREN welcome **DISABLED** access difficult
PETS accepted by arrangement
CLOSED Nov-Mar
PROPRIETOR Francis Noel-Baker

NORTH-EAST AEGEAN ISLANDS

MAVROKORDATIKO
~ TRADITIONAL GUESTHOUSE ~

82100 Kambos, Chios
TEL 0271 32900 FAX 0271 32902 E-MAIL kambos@compulink.gr

A DEEP BLUE POOL that reflects the columns and stone archways of this lovely 18thC mansion is one of the most abiding impressions of this place. Built in 1736 by one of Chios's wealthiest aristocratic Byzantine families, it was gifted to the municipality of Chios by the last member of the Mavrokordatos dynasty in 1938.

Many of its original features remain in place, such as the pebbled courtyard, the great water cistern, and the typically Chiot mangano wheel which was used to draw water from the cistern. A stay here takes you back to the era of the great families of Chios, and the rooms retain many period fittings, although they are also comfortable, with modern luxuries. The café and restaurant serve excellent local delicacies. Service is amiable, but perhaps not quite as slick and professional as it might be.

Located between Chios town and the island's airport, Mavrokordatiko is a useful base from which to explore the island, but is perhaps better suited to a short stay than a long week's or fortnight's holiday. With its quiet setting, within a 6 hectare farming estate, it would be an ideal choice for families with young children.

~

NEARBY Chios town.
LOCATION 7 km from town, 3 km from airport
FOOD breakfast, lunch, dinner, snacks
PRICE €€
ROOMS 9 double with phone, TV, minibar, radio
FACILITIES garden, swimming pool
CREDIT CARDS not accepted
CHILDREN welcome
DISABLED access difficult
PETS accepted
CLOSED Nov-Mar
MANAGER Dimitris Kitrilakis

NORTH-EAST AEGEAN ISLANDS

VOLISSOS, CHIOS

TA PETRINA

~ RESTORED VILLAGE HOUSES ~

Volissos, Chios
TEL 0274 21128 FAX 0274 21013 E-MAIL tapetrina@chi.forthnet.gr

THESE BEAUTIFULLY RESTORED HOUSES in one of the most charming and unspoiled villages on Chios are the result of a partnership between English carpenter Patrick Witham, his partner Maria and a local Greek builder, Michaelis. Between them they have renovated a selection of village houses, with accommodation ranging from studios for two to whole houses sleeping up to ten people and so perfect for families and groups of friends. They are also very affordably priced. Patrick and Michaelis have taken great care to retain a traditional feel, but the houses are well equipped with modern facilities including washing machines and electric cookers. Some houses are accessible by car, and some rooms have a proper bathtub as well as the more usual shower room.

The houses include Panayotis House, a spacious stone-built property suitable for families, with spectacular views from its terraces; the cosy Zarta House, sleeping two to three people; and the large Lagos House, which can be rented as a whole for groups of up to ten people, or as two independent properties, the Little House and the Garden House. Maria, an interior designer, has decorated all the rooms in keeping with the traditional styles and motifs of the island.

~

NEARBY Genoese castle; Volissos village
LOCATION 35 km NW of Chios town
FOOD self catering
PRICE ©©©
ROOMS 5 double with en suite or attached shower or bath; 3 twin; 1 double with separate shower room; 1 studio; 4 sofa beds
FACILITIES garden, terraces
CREDIT CARDS MC, V
CHILDREN welcome
DISABLED some ground-floor bedrooms
PETS accepted by arrangement CLOSED Nov-Mar
MANAGER Patrick Witham

SPORADES

PLATANIAS, SKIATHOS

ATRIUM HOTEL

RESORT HOTEL

37002 Platanias, Skiathos

TEL 0427 49345
FAX 0427 49444
FOOD breakfast, dinner
PRICE €€€€
CLOSED Nov-Mar
PROPRIETORS Tourist Enterprises Atrium SA

THIS PURPOSE-BUILT LUXURY HOTEL has 75 rooms. Unlike most resort hotels on this popular island of pine forests and golden sand beaches, it has been imaginatively designed and constructed using traditional materials (mainly pine and local stone), and blends in with its surroundings on pine-clad slopes above Platanias, one of the best beaches on Skiathos. It is only a 100 m walk to the beach, but for those too relaxed to make even this short journey, there is also an attractive swimming pool with lovely views and a terrace bar. This is a hotel built mainly with the package holiday-maker in mind, and its restaurant only offers a buffet, but the many *tavernas* and excellent restaurants of Skiathos town are only a 9 km taxi or bus ride away.

CHORA, SKIATHOS

CARNAYIO

TOWN RESTAURANT

Paralia, Chora

TEL 0427 22868
PRICE €€€
CREDIT CARDS MC, V
CLOSED Nov-Apr

DEFINITELY BOOK AHEAD for dinner at this, the island's best restaurant, which has won praise from numerous food-conscious magazines for its blend of fine cooking and traditional Greek dishes. Dinner here will be memorable, and there is certainly no better place to spend your last evening on Skiathos. The wine list is exceptional, and the menu has original dishes such as *rigatoni* with smoked salmon, *penne* with parma ham, and pepper steak as well as fine seafood including *langouste* and the best of grilled fresh fish. Seating is mainly outdoors, at street level, under a thatched canopy on a paved patio, but there are also some tables inside for use in cooler weather.

SPORADES

HOTEL MATO
VILLAGE HOTEL

30, Odos 25 Martiou, 37002
Skiathos

TEL 0427 22186
FAX 0427 23105
PRICE €€€
CREDIT CARDS MC, V
CLOSED never
PROPRIETOR Angeliki Kotsoridou

LOCATED ON A very quiet pedestrian street in the older part of Skiathos's main village, next to a row of old-fashioned whitewashed cottages, Hotel Mato is small, affordable, friendly and cheerful. It is an old, recently renovated island house, undistinguished but inoffensively decorated, with red-painted woodwork, white walls, and shared balconies running along the front of the second storey. In front is a small courtyard crammed with potted plants and pleasantly scented with jasmine. Inside, it is much more luxurious than you might expect from its unpretentious exterior. The bedrooms are a comfortable blend of modern and traditional, with parquet floors, large built-in wardrobes, striped rugs and large twin or double beds.

TO STEKI
HARBOURSIDE RESTAURANT

Old port, Skiathos

TEL 0427 22474
PRICE €€
CREDIT CARDS MC, V
CLOSED Nov-Mar

THE FIRST OF A ROW of restaurants lining a cobbled lane above the harbour, with attractive views of the bay and the decorative Bourtzi islet, To Steki is a long-standing favourite of ours, with its blue wooden tables and chairs under awnings and friendly, unusually prompt service. It serves good grilled meat and fish dishes, cooked over charcoal, including lobster, prawns, squid and other favourites, and the 'kalavia' fish soup, a Steki speciality, is a treat (and a meal in itself). It also serves pizza, spaghetti, and other popular dishes. For cheap and cheerful open air dining in the middle of this lively little harbour and holiday town, To Steki is one of the best choices.

SPORADES

KANAPITSA, SKIATHOS

KANAPITSA TAVERNA
BEACH TAVERNA

Kanapitsa Beach, 37002 Skiathos

TEL 0427 24191
PRICE €€€
CREDIT CARDS not accepted
CLOSED Nov-Apr

DEFINITELY NO JACKET required at this amiable beach *taverna* which earns its mention here as much for its fine location on a sandy crescent of beach, well off the road, as for its food, which is run-of-the-mill grilled meat and chicken dishes and good seafood. The restaurant is only 100 m from the Plaza Hotel, making it a handy alternative for those guests who do not want to eat in every night, but do not want to travel into Chora for dinner. It's right on the beach, so parents who want to linger longer over lunch can dispatch children to play within sight. This beach also has a range of water sports, including windsurfer rental, for active teenagers.

PLATANIAS, SKIATHOS

PLAZA HOTEL
RESORT HOTEL

37002 Platanias, Skiathos
TEL 0427 21971
FAX 0427 22109
E-MAIL plaza@n-skiathos.gr
PRICE €€€€
CREDIT CARDS AE, MC
CLOSED Nov-Apr
PROPRIETORS Plaza Hotel SA

ON AN ISLAND where hotels purpose-built for package holiday companies predominate, the Plaza Hotel is one of the better choices. Only ten minutes by road from the little island capital and 15 minutes from the airport, it is handily located, only a few steps from one of Skiathos's many fine sandy beaches, peaceful and well away from the main road, making it a good spot for a family holiday.

The Plaza, whose low-rise building sits in a natural amphitheatre of wooded slopes, has a large pool. Inside, the atrium-style lobby is cool and shady, with a small cocktail/piano bar, and a large breakfast room on a sunny terrace.

Upstairs, the bedrooms are bland, ordinarily equipped, serviced and decorated to the standards you would expect from a mid-to-upper range holiday hotel.

NORTH-EAST AEGEAN ISLANDS

VESSA, CHIOS

TO PETRINO
VILLAGE GUESTHOUSE

82100 Vessa, Chios

TEL 0271 73320
FAX 0271 73320
E-MAIL nmereos@chi.forthnet.gr
FOOD breakfast, dinner
PRICE €
CLOSED Nov-Mar
PROPRIETOR Nestoras Mereos

To PETRINO STANDS AMONG traditional village homes in the middle of Vessa, one of Chios's famous medieval mastic villages. A substantial, two-storey stone house, built in 1874 by one of the more prosperous villagers, it has been transformed into a comfortable guesthouse, with large rooms, furnished and decorated with local textiles and antique furniture. This is a useful base for exploring the island, and will appeal to people who like walking and cycling and are not looking for a busy beach resort, though there are sandy and pebbly beaches only 6 km away. Home-cooked food is part of the attraction, and the quiet village also has a selection of traditional *tavernas* and cafés.

ARMENISTIS, IKARIA

CAVOS BAY
SEASIDE HOTEL

83301 Armenistis, Ikaria

TEL 0275 71381
FAX 0275 71380
E-MAIL cavos_bay@ika.forthnet.gr
FOOD buffet breakfast, lunch, dinner **PRICE** €€€
CLOSED never
PROPRIETOR Emmanolis Rigas

THIS WAS THE FIRST PROPER HOTEL in a friendly little village near a splendid beach, and has been a well-kept secret until recently. It is still one of the best hotels on the island, not only for its attractive location – on a rocky cape just outside the village, with dazzling sea views and sunsets – but for its high standards of design and excellent facilities. Built in six tiers, the hotel is unobtrusive and, as its grounds mature, it is becoming a green oasis, with bougainvillea, eucalyptus and cypresses softening the building's outlines. The beach is a ten minute walk away, but there are two sea-water pools overlooking the Aegean. Service is friendly (though the staff is not numerous) and facilities are up-to-the-minute. It can be busy in summer.

SOUTHERN AEGEAN

AREA INTRODUCTION

THE SOUTHERN AEGEAN ISLANDS are the best known and best loved of Greek isles, and are officially divided into two administrative areas: the numerous,and mostly tiny, Cyclades, scattered across a roughly circular area of sea between Crete and the mainland, and the Dodecanese, a crescent chain of a dozen isles not far from the Turkish coast.

The Cyclades are the islands that most visitors tend to think of as quintessentially Greek, with whitewashed villages of tiny, one-storey houses, dazzlingly bright in the summer sun, and tiny blue-domed churches dotted across rocky hillsides, bare but for a few olive trees. They are also the island-hopper's favourites, with frequent and short connections by ferry and hydrofoil between islands that often lie in sight of each other.

Getting there no longer requires a long ferry trip from Piraeus (the port of Athens) as there are frequent domestic flights from Athens to many of the Cyclades, as well as summer charter flights to the most popular Cycladic islands, Mikonos and Santorini, and to Rhodes, Kos and Karpathos in the Dodecanese. On most routes, high-speed catamarans and hydrofoils also supplement the slower, cheaper conventional ferries.

Although the Cyclades are superficially similar, each has its own character, atmosphere and distinctive island architecture. We have found a plethora of charming small hotels on three of the most popular islands - trendy Mikonos, friendly Paros, and stunningly scenic Santorini – and on a couple of smaller, less well-known isles. Mikonos has perhaps the widest choice – from elegant boutique hotels in the centre of its charming main village, to some of Greece's most sought after small luxury hotels – while Santorini's unique cliffside hotels have world-class views. Paros, cheerful and unpretentious with some great beaches, also has a wide range of charming places to stay for a rather wider range of budgets than its neighbours.

In the Dodecanese,the large island of Rhodes has some delightful hotels within and near the walls of Europe's most intact medieval city, and we have also found a handful of charming family-run properties on tiny Simi, a short ferry ride from Rhodes.

Very few hotels in the Cyclades stay open in winter, though there are some exceptions on Mikonos. The islands are definitely at their pleasantest in early summer – Easter to mid-June and in autumn (September to mid-October), – while the peak summer months of July and August (when the islands are at their most crowded) are really for serious sunworshippers only.

ARGO-SARONIC ISLANDS

IDRA

HOTEL DELFINI

~ ISLAND HOTEL ~

18040 Idra
TEL 0298 52082

A BOVE A PAVEMENT CAFÉ, whose white canvas chairs and marble tables spill out over the quayside, the Hotel Delfini could not be handier (or better value) for those arriving off the ferry from Athens and looking for a cheap and cheerful place to stay on Idra.

Its dazzling white walls are set off by vivid blue-painted woodwork, and steep marble steps lead up to the reception area on the first floor, where a large model of an island schooner hangs on the wall and the earthly remains of the mother of all lobsters lurks in a glass case.

The Delfini is much bigger than it appears from outside, with rooms on two floors – those on the lower floor, one storey up from the quayside, have the better views, but those on the upper floor, set back from the harbour, are quieter. Rooms are smallish, but simple and clean, with tiled floors and pine beds.

This is a hotel for those who really like the hustle and bustle of a busy quayside lined with cafés and who do not mind staying up late (things don't quieten down outside until well after midnight, and the first ferries arrive early). That said, Euro for Euro, this is among the best places to stay on Idra.

~

NEARBY Idra village; island beaches.
LOCATION quayside in centre of village
FOOD breakfast
PRICE €€
ROOMS 11 twin, all with WC and shower
FACILITIES breakfast room
CREDIT CARDS not accepted
CHILDREN not suitable
DISABLED not suitable
PETS not accepted
CLOSED never
PROPRIETOR Giorgios T. Saitis

ARGO-SARONIC ISLANDS

IDRA

HOTEL HYDRA
~ ISLAND HOTEL ~

18040 Idra
TEL and FAX 0298 52102 E-MAIL hydrahotel@aig.forthnet.gr

THIS HOTEL IS NOT HARD TO FIND – whereas some of Idra's hotels and pensions are tucked away in the village's maze of pedestrian lanes, the Hydra is high above the harbour and easy to spot as soon as you get off the ferry. The downside is that it is a steep, uphill hike from sea level up to this solid, two-storey stone mansion with its tall windows and central balcony looking out over one of the prettiest harbour villages in the Aegean. The up side is that the Hydra certainly has the best views in town, and at what are, by Idra island standards, affordable rates.

Big clumps of greenery swarm over the front of the building beside the front door, which opens off a narrow cobbled lane into a ground-floor lobby with high ceilings, white stucco walls and a cool stone floor. This room sets the tone for the whole place, which is simple, clean, and friendly, with high-ceilinged bedrooms, simply decorated and sunny. All in all, the Hydra is the best value for money on an island which is notably short of value-for-money accommodation. It also makes a useful base for those who may want to explore the sights and museums of Athens (an easy day-trip by hydrofoil) but who do not want to stay in the grime, noise and traffic of the big city

~

NEARBY harbour; island beaches.
LOCATION above harbour, Idra village
FOOD breakfast
PRICE €€€
ROOMS 12 double, all with en suite shower and WC
FACILITIES sitting room, bar
CREDIT CARDS V
CHILDREN not suitable
DISABLED not suitable
PETS not accepted
CLOSED never
PROPRIETOR Dimitris Davis

ARGO-SARONIC ISLANDS

POROS

STO ROLOI
～ TRADITIONAL APARTMENTS ～

18020 Poros
TEL 0298 25808 **FAX** 0298 9345775 **E-MAIL** storoloi@hotmail.com

STO ROLOI IS A REAL FIND. The owner, an Austrian architect, well-known for her expertise in renovating medieval buildings, restored this one in 1999. She has created three comfortable self-contained apartments in a 200-year-old stone-built island house; you can rent any one of them separately or, for a large group, take the whole house. Elaborately carved wooden doors at the entrance set the tone for the whole property, and the massively thick stone walls provide natural air conditioning, keeping the house cool in summer and cosy in winter. All the rooms are tastefully decorated with a mix of island antiques, including round wooden tables, heavy old wooden armchairs, bench seats and prints, and more modern furnishings.

Sto Roloi stands next to the picturesque clock tower from which it gets its name, in a quiet corner of lively Poros town, but close to the shops, restaurants and cafés around the harbour. There is a handy wrought-iron balcony from which you can watch the sun set over the harbour and the yachts anchored just below. Sto Roloi would be a good base for day trips to Epidavros and other ancient sights of the Argolid peninsula; the mainland is only a few hundred metres away and there are frequent 'water-taxis' which will take you to nearby island beaches.

～

NEARBY Poros town; beaches.
LOCATION close to centre of Poros town, 25 m from harbour
FOOD self-catering
PRICE €€€
ROOMS 2 4-bed apartments, 1 2-bed room, all with en-suite WC and shower, kitchen; first-floor apartment also has sauna and hydromassage bath
FACILITIES sitting rooms, balcony, garden
CREDIT CARDS MC, V
CHILDREN welcome
DISABLED access to ground-floor garden studio
PETS accepted by arrangement **CLOSED** never
PROPRIETOR Maria Louisa Andoniadou

Argo-Saronic Islands

Dapia, Spetses

Zoe's Club

~ Island resort ~

Dapia, 18050 Spetses
Tel 0298 74447 **Fax** 0298 72841

THIS SECLUDED COMPLEX on the outskirts of Dapia is an excellent choice for families. Part of the complex is in a restored 19thC building, with two adjoining modern buildings, influenced by traditional design. They are built around a courtyard and a huge pool, surrounded by a flower-filled patio garden shaded by fig and olive trees. Wooden pergolas and white poolside umbrellas also provide shelter from the intense summer sun. Traditional island materials – earthenware tiles, slate and terracotta floors, and local marble in bathrooms – add a touch of class.

Each apartment has a small kitchen, large sitting room, and its own terrace and balcony. Special attention has been paid to details such as sound and heat insulation, and the rooms are bright, cool (air conditioned) and quiet. There are views over the pretty village of Dapia (Spetsai's miniature capital) to the sea, not five minutes' walk away. Zoe's Club offers the best of several worlds – classical, stylish design with all the modern facilities you could want; peace and quiet but with the lively harbour area, restaurants, cafés and nightspots on the doorstep.

Nearby Dapia; harbour; island beaches.
Location 300 m from centre of Dapia
Food breakfast, snacks
Price €€€
Rooms 20 apartments with 1-3 bedrooms with en suite WC and shower; all apartments have phone, TV, air conditioning, living room, kitchen, balcony, terrace
Facilities snack bar, swimming pool
Credit cards AE, MC, V
Children welcome
Disabled access possible
Pets accepted by arrangement
Closed never
Proprietors Zoe SA

ARGO-SARONIC ISLANDS

SPETSES

NISSIA HOTEL

~ ISLAND RESORT ~

Kounoupitsa, 18050 Spetses
TEL 0298 75000 **FAX** 0298 75012

THE NISSIA IS A RESORT HOTEL with a difference, incorporating an immaculately restored 1920s neoclassical building (officially listed as one of the island's most important historic buildings) within a modern resort of 31 luxurious apartments, built in the same style. The effect is an elegant complex, which combines period charm with every modern convenience and plenty of privacy.

Painted in pretty pastel colours, the Nissia overlooks the sea, and some apartments have views of the mainland hills and nearby islands. There are three different types of studio and one two-storey house, ideal for families, with two twin-bedded and two double-bedded rooms, plus a sofa-bed on the ground floor. It also has its own balcony and private terrace. The house, and the large studios, all have fireplaces, making them cosy places to stay in spring and autumn.

The jewels of the collection, however, are the two 'presidential' apartments in the two towers of the restored building, reached by interior stairs or a private lift. Each of these is rich in period architectural and design details, has a private verandah with a view of the sea, and sleeps up to six.

~

NEARBY Dapia (Spetses town).
LOCATION 1 km W of harbour
FOOD self-catering
PRICE €€€€
ROOMS 31 apartments sleeping 3-8; all have phone, TV, air conditioning, central heating, daily cleaning service
FACILITIES balconies, courtyard, garden
CREDIT CARDS AE, MC, V
CHILDREN welcome
DISABLED access possible
PETS accepted by arrangement
CLOSED Nov-Mar
PROPRIETORS Dynamic Discovery SA

CYCLADES

CHORA, ANDROS

STAGEIRA HOTEL

~ HILLSIDE HOTEL ~

Dexameni, Chora, Andros
TEL 0282 23525 **FAX** 0282 24502 **E-MAIL** stageira@otenet.gr

T HIS ATTRACTIVE NEW HOTEL is just outside the sleepy main town of Andros, an island which has yet to be over-exploited by international tourism, and is certainly the most stylish place to stay on the island, with two caveats: it is too far to walk into town or to the beach, and, on our inspection, it had no pool (though one is planned for summer 2002, according to the owner). Your own car or motorbike is, therefore, almost essential.

The Stageira compensates with a fantastic hillside position, looking out over a terraced, wooded valley and green pastures where horses graze. Surrounded by bare rocky hills, it reminded one visitor of the American West in miniature. The hotel is in neoclassical style, painted white and lavender-blue, and has a bright and breezy open-plan lobby and reception area leading on to a sunny café-terrace with white umbrellas and black and white marble tables and chairs. Owner-manager Christiana Valmas is equally bright and breezy, and ferociously efficient.

Rooms are all suites, modern in style and furnishing, without being chain-hotel bland, and very well equipped. Off-street parking and a lift specifically designed for wheelchair access also make this hotel an outstanding recommendation.

~

NEARBY Chora; beach; heliport.
LOCATION 1 km outside main island village, on hillside; car parking
FOOD breakfast
PRICE €€€
ROOMS 10 suites with en suite WC and shower; all rooms have air conditioning
FACILITIES lobby sitting area, lift, terrace
CREDIT CARDS MC, V
CHILDREN accepted
DISABLED access possible
PETS accepted by arrangement
CLOSED never
PROPRIETORS Antonis and Christiana Valmas

CYCLADES

ERMOUPOLI, SIROS

ESPERANCE ROOMS AND STUDIOS

~ TOWN HOUSE HOTEL ~

Ermoupoli, Siros
TEL 0281 81671 **FAX** 0281 85707

THIS ELEGANT SMALL HOTEL is a pleasant discovery in Ermoupoli, an island capital neglected by foreign visitors but well liked by Greek holiday-makers. The blue shutters and pink-and-white stucco pilasters of its neo-classical façade lend it a whimsical air. The management and staff are friendly and helpful, and rooms are simply (if rather blandly) furnished and decorated with modern furniture. Two rooms at the front of the hotel have balconies and views of the harbour – though, as those who have visited Siros already know, this is a busy commercial port, not a picturesque fishing harbour.

Being so close to the harbour makes the Esperance ideal for those spending a couple of nights on Siros or one night between changing ferries. The whole of the ground floor, with its arcaded terrace, is taken up by the hotel's own Belle Amie restaurant, which serves breakfast, lunch, and a memorable assortment of *mezedes* in the evening. You would not make a detour to Ermoupoli just to stay at the Esperance; on the other hand, if your itinerary includes a stopover on Siros, then this is definitely the best place to stay near the harbour.

~

NEARBY Siros town; harbour.
LOCATION waterfront, 750 m from ferry harbour
FOOD breakfast, lunch, dinner
PRICE €€
ROOMS 8 twin with en suite WC and shower; all rooms have phone, TV, air conditioning
FACILITIES sitting room, restaurant
CREDIT CARDS not accepted
CHILDREN accepted
DISABLED not suitable
PETS accepted by arrangement
CLOSED never
MANAGER Nikos Voutsinos

CYCLADES

AGIOS STEFANOS, MIKONOS

PRINCESS OF MIKONOS HOTEL
~ RESORT HOTEL ~

84600 Agios Stefanos, Mikonos
TEL 0289 24735 **FAX** 0289 23031 **E-MAIL** princess@myk.forthnet.gr

SITTING ABOVE THE SMALL sandy beach at Agios Stefanos, the Princess of Mikonos faces south, looking towards Chora and the new port at Tourlos. This view is marred at the moment by a new hotel complex being built immediately across the road. The light lobby is well laid out and has the feel of an art gallery, with island antiques such as earthenware jars and wooden furniture, as well as marble carvings and ship models. The lobby also boasts an upmarket jewellery boutique, an offshoot of the owner's shop in town, selling top names such as Cartier, Rolex and Vacheron Constantin.

Rooms are in the boxy white cottages typical of Mikonos, with bright blue woodwork and balconies, and are built around a medium-sized sea-water pool, or on terraces linked by stone stairs and pathways. Rooms have a small entrance and plenty of space, with pine ceilings, reproduction traditional furniture, four-poster beds and large bathrooms with that uncommon luxury in island hotels, a real bathtub. Like the pool, most of the rooms have a fine view out to sea and along the coast. Service and management are friendly and efficient, and despite — or perhaps even because of – its out-of-town location, this is an excellent choice for a stay on Mikonos.

~

NEARBY Agios Stefanos beach; Chora; ports.
LOCATION 150 m from Agios Stefanos beach, 4 km N of Chora
FOOD breakfast, lunch, dinner
PRICE €€€€
ROOMS 38 double with en suite bath; all rooms have TV, radio, air conditioning, minibar
FACILITIES restaurant, gym, swimming pool, pool bar
CREDIT CARDS MC, V
CHILDREN welcome
DISABLED not suitable
PETS not accepted
CLOSED mid-Oct to Apr
PROPRIETOR Theo Roussounelos

CYCLADES

CHORA, MIKONOS

HOTEL BELVEDERE

~ TOWN HOTEL ~

84600 Chora, Mikonos
TEL 0289 25122 **FAX** 0289 25126 **E-MAIL** belvedere@myk.forthnet.gr

THE BELVEDERE IS A NEW five-star hotel on the outskirts of Chora, within a few minutes' walk of the centre but far enough away from the nightlife to escape the after-dark uproar. A recent arrival on the Mikonos scene, it combines modern rooms in new wings, built around an old mansion dating from 1850, which has now been transformed into the hotel's restaurant. A fine pool (and children's pool) have also been added.

The lobby area, with its arches and wooden sofas and deep white armchairs, has French windows which open on to a fabulous terrace overlooking the pool and the white buildings of Chora. The terraces and stone pathways are planted with cypresses and potted palms, and the overall impression is of a tranquil village hideaway. The public areas and restaurant are furnished with graceful wooden tables and chairs in the style of the 19th century.

The bedrooms are well laid out and furnished, and all have great views, tiled floors, and varnished wood ceilings. The colour scheme is predominantly white and blue, with neutral coloured soft furnishings. Staff are young, friendly, and eager to help, and the Belvedere must be among the best hotel choices in Chora.

~

NEARBY port; Chora; beaches; Delos.
LOCATION Rohari district, outskirts of Chora, 500 m from harbour, 1 km from ferry port; car parking
FOOD breakfast, lunch, dinner; room service
PRICE €€€€
ROOMS 46; 40 double, 6 suites, all with bath, hairdrier, phone, fax and internet, air conditioning, TV, video, minibar and balcony with sea view
FACILITIES restaurant, bar, fitness room, swimming pool, laundry
CREDIT CARDS AE, DC, MC, V
CHILDREN welcome (babysitting available)
DISABLED access difficult
PETS not accepted
CLOSED Jan, Feb
PROPRIETORS Semeli Hotel Mikonos

CYCLADES

CHORA, MIKONOS

HOTEL ELENA

~ TOWN HOTEL ~

84600 Chora, Mikonos
TEL 0289 23457 **FAX** 0289 23458

THIS SIMPLE, CHEERFUL LITTLE HOTEL (under the same ownership as the Apollonia Bay at Agios Ioannis) is a welcome addition to the limited choice of value for money hotels in Chora. With its varnished pine beams and whitewashed walls, it echoes the traditional architecture of the island, and the rooms on the upper floor of the two-storey building have bright blue shutters which open on to charming wooden balconies.

Breakfast can be taken in the surprisingly stylish arched breakfast room-cum-bar, or outside on a sunny terrace beside a pedestrian street (the smart and expensive Belvedere and Semeli hotels are immediately opposite, so for a treat you could eat dinner in either of their commendable restaurants). The staff are friendly and helpful and can organize car or motorbike rental, or day trips across the bay to the ancient ruins of Delos. The rooms are charming (especially the suites which have canopied wooden four-poster beds), with Klee prints on the walls, varnished wood floors and some fine examples of antique furniture from prosperous 19thC homes, of which this was one. There is no pool, but guests may use the one at the Hotel Anastasios, only five minutes' walk away. Unlike most hotels on Mikonos, the Elena is open year round.

~

NEARBY Chora; harbour; ferry port; Delos; beaches.
LOCATION Rohari district, outskirts of Chora, 500 m from harbour, 1 km from ferry port
FOOD breakfast
PRICE €€€
ROOMS 28 double and twin with en suite WC and shower; all rooms have phone, TV, air conditioning, hairdrier
FACILITIES breakfast room/bar, fax, safe deposit
CREDIT CARDS AE, MC, V
CHILDREN not suitable
DISABLED not suitable **PETS** not accepted **CLOSED** never
PROPRIETORS Apollonia Bay SA

CYCLADES

CHORA, MIKONOS

HOTEL ROCHARI

~ TOWN HOTEL ~

84600 Chora, Mikonos
TEL 0289 23107 **FAX** 0289 24307 **E-MAIL** rochari@otenet.gr

SIMPLE, CHEAP and cheerful, this small hotel close to the centre of Chora is handily located but escapes the thumping disco beat that makes it hard to get a good night's sleep in most small hotels closer to the centre of one of the Aegean's nightlife hot spots. The management is very friendly, and the public areas and rooms are well and unfussily designed, in the style of a Mikonos home, with wooden shutters, a varnished pine ceiling, and marble floors.

The medium-sized pool is well situated, overlooked by a pleasant café terrace where you can sit gazing over the rooftops of the labyrinthine village while enjoying a drink as the sun sets.

Located on the main road that circles the town, the Rochari is accessible by car and has off-street parking. A downside is that there is some traffic noise, especially in the rooms at the back, but this seems a fair trade-off for some peace and quiet in the small hours.

Flowers and greenery make the pathways and small garden very pleasant, and overall the Rochari offers excellent value for money and an ideal location for those who want to stay in or near the centre of Chora.

~

NEARBY Chora; Delos; beaches.
LOCATION outskirts of Chora, 500 m from harbour, 1 km from ferry port
FOOD breakfast, snacks
PRICE €€€
ROOMS 60 twin or double, all with en suite shower, WC, TV, phone
FACILITIES restaurant, bar, swimming pool
CREDIT CARDS MC, V
CHILDREN accepted
DISABLED not suitable
PETS not accepted
CLOSED Nov-Mar
PROPRIETOR P. Koussathanas

CYCLADES

CHORA, MIKONOS

SEMELI HOTEL

~ VILLAGE HOTEL ~

84600 Chora, Mikonos
TEL 0289 27466 FAX 0289 27467 E-MAIL semeliht@otenet.gr

THE SEMELI IS SIMPLY delightful, and is our favourite hotel on Mikonos. It was built in 1996, with an old Chora mansion as its core, around which has been constructed a Cycladic village of two-storey houses with green and blue woodwork, wooden balconies, shaded verandahs and stone-paved paths. The reception area, in the hall of the old building, is gorgeous, with a patterned tile floor, whitewashed rafters, antique furniture from the original home, and fresh bouquets and wreaths of bougainvillea flowers in niches and on the wall. Typical island motifs are incorporated throughout, such as the pattern of niches in the wall by the bar, reminiscent of a Cycladic dovecot. The vaulted bar area has stone shelves and niches and a large open fireplace for cooler evenings. It is furnished with comfortable sofas and armchairs, and light streams in through large windows.

The restaurant is now regarded as one of the best in Chora for its traditional and Mediterranean cooking, and the hotel even has its own tiny chapel to St George. The pool is substantial, and the pool bar very congenial at any time. The same sense of style and attention to detail is carried through to the bedrooms, each of which has its own colour scheme in mellow checked, striped and floral patterns, with polished wood or tiled floors.

~

NEARBY Chora; port; beaches; Delos.
LOCATION outskirts of Chora, 500 m from harbour, 1 km from ferry port; car parking
FOOD breakfast, lunch, dinner
PRICE €€€€
ROOMS 42 doubles, 3 suites, all with en suite WC and shower; all rooms have phone, TV, air conditioning, minibar, balcony or verandah.
FACILITIES restaurant, fitness centre, Jacuzzi, swimming pool, pool bar, laundry, fax service, safe deposit
CREDIT CARDS AE, MC, V
CHILDREN welcome (babysitting available) **DISABLED** access difficult
PETS not accepted **CLOSED** Nov-Mar **PROPRIETOR** Semeli Hotel Mikonos

CYCLADES

Chora, Mikonos

ZORZIS HOTEL

~ Town house hotel ~

30 N. Kalogera, 84600 Chora, Mikonos
Tel 0289 22167 **Fax** 0289 24169 **e-mail** zorzis@otenet.gr

AN EXCITING NEW find in Chora is this charming little family home, run as a hotel for some 30 years but recently given a new 'boutique-hotel' look by Australian-Greek owner, Jonathan Varnalis. Zorzis is on a relatively quiet, pedestrian street in the middle of Chora (most of the other buildings are shops, not bars, and those to the rear of the hotel are private homes, so it is quite quiet at night). Its individual style is evident inside and out. Greek antiques and icons on the stairway and in the corridor mingle with original graphic artwork. Beds have patchwork quilts and the (admittedly tiny) shower rooms have black and white tiles and chrome fittings for an Art Deco look.

There is a simple sun-deck on the roof and a shared balcony to the front of the hotel, and the two suites each have a private balcony. To the rear of the building is a terrace, shaded by vines, which backs on to the tiny gardens of neighbouring houses, and there are a couple of round café tables at the front of the hotel, beside Kalogera Street. The British manager, Joanna Wade, is very friendly, professional and helpful, and the Zorzis is excellent value for money compared with most Mikonos hotels.

~

Nearby Chora; harbour; ferry port; beaches; Delos.
Location pedestrian street in town centre
Food breakfast
Price €€
Rooms 10; 4 double, 4 twin, all with en suite WC and shower, 1 suite with 1 bed, 1 suite with 2 beds, both with shared WC and shower
Facilities bar, roof terrace
Credit cards MC, V
Children not suitable
Disabled not suitable
Pets not accepted
Closed Jan-Feb
Proprietor Jonathan Varnalis

CYCLADES

KALO LIVADI, MIKONOS

PIETRA E MARE SUITES

~ ISLAND HOTEL ~

84600 Kalo Livadi, Mikonos
TEL *0289 71152* **FAX** *0289 71441*

THIS SMALL MODERN complex of apartments in stone and plaster cottages stands in glorious isolation high above one of the island's best and least crowded beaches, at the end of a very rough dirt road. Local stone has been used extensively, while its hard edges are softened by masses of bougainvillea and other shrubs. The small but adequate pool occupies most of a lower terrace, with the apartment cottages rising in two tiers above it, and with views of a deep blue and turquoise bay.

Service is amiable but unobtrusive and the rooms combine typical island touches, such as gallery beds, with modern facilities, although some of the rooms give the impression of having been furnished as cheaply as possible. The Pietra e Mare's interior decoration does not match up to its seductive exterior. Everything works, but this is not a hotel for style purists. However, some guests (families with small children, perhaps) may find it an unpretentious and refreshing change from the self-consciously stylish 'boutique hotels' which are becoming more common on many of the Cyclades.

~

NEARBY Kalo Livadi beach.
LOCATION above beach (steep dirt road), 13 km from Chora on S coast
FOOD breakfast, snacks, self-catering
PRICE €€€
ROOMS 19 suites with double or twin beds plus sofa bed; all suites have phone, TV, air conditioning, minibar, kitchen
FACILITIES 2 bars, swimming pool
CREDIT CARDS MC, V
CHILDREN welcome
DISABLED not suitable
PETS accepted by arrangement
CLOSED Oct-Mar
PROPRIETOR Eleni Stavrakopoulou

CYCLADES

KOLIMBITHRES, PAROS

HOTEL KOUROS

～ RESORT HOTEL ～

84400 Kolimbithres, Paros
TEL 0284 51000 **FAX** 0284 51688 **E-MAIL** info@hotelkouros.gr

THIS BEAUTIFULLY KEPT, quiet hotel has a low-rise, Cycladic design: two-storey white houses, with brightly painted woodwork, are set among lawns, surrounding a two-storey main building. The pool, bordered by a stone-paved patio, is in front of the main building, and the sandy beach at Kolimbithres is an easy 150 m walk. A copy of the Paros *kouros* (marble statue of a youth), after which the hotel is named, stands in the cool, partially open-air lobby. Service is low-key but friendly, and the rooms, though not outstandingly original in their decoration, are comfortable and well equipped. Each room has its own balcony or terrace, with views of the sea, the surrounding hills or fields.

The Kouros is unpretentious. It has all the facilities of a proper little resort hotel. With fewer than 100 beds it rarely gets crowded even in summer, and it has none of the ostentation and pretensions to grand hotel status of the nearby Astir. It also represents great value for money, especially for a family holiday. Naoussa is (just) within walking distance, but the hotel's minibus will take you to this village, and to Parikia, the island's main port.

～

NEARBY Naoussa; Parikia; beach.
LOCATION 150 m from beach, 2.5 km from Naoussa village; car parking
FOOD breakfast, lunch, dinner, snacks
PRICE €€€
ROOMS 54; 40 double, 10 single, 4 suites, all with private WC and shower; all rooms have phone, TV, radio, balcony or verandah; some rooms have air conditioning
FACILITIES restaurant, 2 bars, garden, swimming pool
CREDIT CARDS MC, V
CHILDREN welcome
DISABLED access to some ground-floor rooms
PETS accepted **CLOSED** Nov-Mar
PROPRIETORS Hotel Kouros

CYCLADES

CHRISI AKTI, PAROS

POSEIDON OF PAROS

~ LUXURY HOTEL AND APARTMENT COMPLEX ~

84400 Chrisi Akti, Paros
TEL 0284 42650 **FAX** 0284 42649 **E-MAIL** poseidon@otenet.gr

THIS WELL-PLACED COMPLEX, with its white, modern-Cycladic houses over-looking Paros's best beach and with great views out to sea and to the hills of Naxos opposite, is remarkably reasonably priced for what it offers. Visit in the shoulder months (May and September) and a stay here will be a real bargain.

Rolling green lawns, well kept and dotted here and there with the palm trees that have become so popular on Paros, surround the Poseidon's simple yet elegant buildings, and there is a huge, dazzlingly blue pool above the beach. There is a poolside restaurant as well as a breakfast room, so the complex combines the benefits of simple self-catering with full service. Apartments and different-sized suites with convertible sofa beds sleep two or four, making this one of the best options for a family holiday on Paros. For families with active teenage children, there is a wide choice of water sports at Chrisi Akti, a particular favourite with windsurfers.

~

NEARBY Chrisi Akti beach; Naoussa; Parikia.
LOCATION Cape Chori, N end of long sandy beach, 18 km from Parikia; car parking
FOOD breakfast, lunch, dinner
PRICE €€ - €€€
ROOMS 20 apartments for 2-4, 10 suites for 2-4; all have phone, TV, air conditioning, hairdrier, safe, sea view, basic kitchenette
FACILITIES restaurant, garden, swimming pools, tennis, laundry, car rental
CREDIT CARDS AE, DC, MC, V
CHILDREN welcome
DISABLED access possible
PETS accepted by arrangement
CLOSED Oct-Apr
PROPRIETORS Poseidon of Paros

CYCLADES

LEFKES, PAROS

LEFKES VILLAGE

VILLAGE HOTEL

84400 Lefkes, Paros
TEL 0284 42398 **FAX** 0284 41827

THE MOST INDIVIDUAL and interesting hotel on Paros is set high in the hills in the typically Cycladic, 16thC village of Lefkes. Owner George Pittas has created a stunningly attractive hotel which blends neoclassical and vernacular island architecture in a building of real character. There is a fine, medium-sized pool with its own bar and a surrounding sunbathing terrace with wonderful views down the valley to the sea and the neighbouring island of Naxos. The staff are very friendly, and the village itself is one of the prettiest on Paros, with several pleasant *tavernas* and cafés.

The Lefkes Village has every modern facility, and the bedrooms are stylishly simple, but it is the owner's fascination with culture and local tradition that makes it a really interesting and unusual place to stay. In the basement area is Mr Pittas's beautifully designed and displayed Museum of Popular Aegean Civilization, with collections of everything from pebbles and wild flowers to traditional pottery, tools and farm implements, chairs and tableware. Who would have thought that there could be so many variations, from different islands, on the basic wooden chair? The museum is a sad reminder of how much of the rich variety and folklore of the islands has been lost.

NEARBY Lefkes village; Chrisi Akti beach; Parikia.
LOCATION 750 m from village centre, down a steep hill
FOOD breakfast, lunch, dinner; room service
PRICE €€€
ROOMS 20 rooms including 18 double, 2 triple, all with en suite WC and shower; all rooms have phone, air conditioning, minibar
FACILITIES bar, restaurant, museum, garden, swimming pool, pool bar
CREDIT CARDS MC, V
CHILDREN welcome
DISABLED not suitable
PETS accepted by arrangement **CLOSED** Nov-Mar
PROPRIETOR George Pittas

CYCLADES

HOTEL AKTAION
∼ ISLAND VILLAGE HOTEL ∼

84400 Logaras, Paros
TEL 0284 41098 **FAX** 0284 41733
WEBSITE www.greek-tourism.gr/aktaion-paros

THIS CHEAP AND CHEERFUL, family-run hotel, right on the small sandy beach in the lively little resort and fishing village of Logaras, is surrounded by tall eucalyptus trees. A tall arched stone doorway leads into an inner court-yard surrounded by simple white buildings with blue-painted woodwork and balconies, most of which overlook the sea. There is also a marvellous sea view from the simple roof terrace.

The rooms are plain and on the small side, with the minimum of furniture, and the owners clearly assume – and rightly – that their clients will be spending most of their waking hours on the beach or in the equally amiable *taverna* which occupies the ground floor facing the beach. For those in search of a little more space, the Aktaion also has two-room apartments with their own kitchens. The reason we decided to include the Aktaion in this guide, however, was the friendliness of the helpful owners, and the fact that it has two ground-floor rooms specifically designed for wheelchair users, with wooden ramps from street level (two steps down) and extra large shower rooms. Very few Greek hotels in this price category respond so well to the needs of people with disabilities.

∼

NEARBY Logaras beach; village; Naoussa; Parikia.
LOCATION on beach, 100 m from village centre; car parking
FOOD breakfast, lunch, dinner
PRICE €
ROOMS 16 twin, 2 studios with kitchenette, all with air conditioning, shower, fridge, WC, TV, phone, balcony or verandah with sea view; 2 rooms with wheelchair access
FACILITIES sitting room, TV room, café-bar, restaurant
CREDIT CARDS MC, V
CHILDREN welcome
DISABLED 2 specially adapted rooms
PETS accepted by arrangement **CLOSED** Oct-May
PROPRIETORS Theodoris and Katerina Melanitis

CYCLADES

PISSO LIVADI, PAROS

ELENA STUDIOS AND APARTMENTS

~ ISLAND VILLAGE HOTEL ~

84400 Pisso Livadi, Paros
TEL 0284 41082 **FAX** 0284 41139

O N A QUIET HILLSIDE just 50 m from Logaras beach and the lively village centre, the Cycladic-style houses of the Elena studios have dazzling whitewashed walls, smart green- and blue-painted woodwork, stone archways that lead into the centre of the low-rise complex, and a briskly friendly, American-Greek manager. Old earthenware olive jars decorate odd corners and wall niches, and all the rooms have sunny verandahs. The Elena really needs a pool to make it perfect, and the management tells us that one is planned, hopefully for 2002, and if not, for 2003.

Some studios can be linked to provide two-bedroom family apartments, and all have basic kitchen equipment (two electric plates, cooker, full set of utensils and tableware). Inside the rooms the furnishings are entirely modern, with tiled floors and comfortable beds; these are undeniably functional rooms, fine for sleeping, but not spaces in which you would wish to linger. Fortunately, the beach beckons. The Elena offers comfort, value for money and friendly efficiency, and its immaculate, traditional exterior more than makes up for any blandness in the interior design.

~

NEARBY Logaras beach; Chrisi Akti; Naoussa; Parikia.
LOCATION 100 m from harbour, on hillside at entrance to village; car parking
FOOD self catering
PRICE ⓔⓔ
ROOMS 29 twin-bedded studios, 1 apartment with 2 beds, all with en suite WC and shower; all have phone, TV, air conditioning, fridge, kitchenette, balcony
FACILITIES terraces
CREDIT CARDS MC, V
CHILDREN welcome
DISABLED not suitable
PETS accepted by arrangement
CLOSED Oct-Mar
PROPRIETOR Angelos Agouros

CYCLADES

NAOUSSA, PAROS

CHROMA HOTEL

~ ISLAND HOTEL ~

84401 Naoussa, Paros
TEL 0284 52690 **FAX** 0284 51630 **E-MAIL** ch@otenet.gr

O N THE OUTSKIRTS OF the resort village of Naoussa, the Chroma Hotel is quiet (apart from the local cockerels whose crowing may wake you early if you leave your bedroom window open). It is the best of a clutch of small hotels set in fields about 500 m from the sea, and around 1 km from the village centre. Although it is modern, it is in the true Cycladic style, with white, cubist buildings, attractive exposed stonework in the surrounding walls and around the pool, and dressed with a mass of potted greenery.

The hotel will have doubled in size by summer 2002, when new rooms will be finished, together with a wing of self-contained one- and two-storey luxury houses which combine traditional architecture with modern facilities. Around this new part of the hotel are well-laid-out patio gardens and, when the palm trees, bougainvillea and cacti mature, this will be an oasis indeed, with its own swimming pool. A new, full-service restaurant will join the snack bar and breakfast restaurant of the original Chroma building.

~

NEARBY Naoussa; beaches.
LOCATION 1 km E of village centre
FOOD breakfast, snacks; lunch and dinner from summer 2002
PRICE €€€
ROOMS 41; 21 twin in original wing, 20 twin in new wing, all with en suite WC and shower; all rooms have phone, TV, air conditioning, minibar, balcony or verandah; 9 houses (3 with 4 beds and loft, 3 with 4 beds, 3 single-storey)
FACILITIES snack bar, restaurant (opening 2002), 2 swimming pools
CREDIT CARDS MC, V
CHILDREN welcome
DISABLED 1 specially adapted house
PETS accepted by arrangement
CLOSED Nov-Mar
PROPRIETORS Chroma Epichirisis AE

CYCLADES

NAOUSSA, PAROS

PETRES HOTEL

~ RESORT HOTEL ~

84401 Naoussa, Paros
TEL 0284 52589 FAX 0284 52759 E-MAIL petres@otenet.gr

THE APPROACH TO this hotel is a little off-putting, as it involves driving for some 200 m up a rough and unsurfaced road through fields. Persevere, because the hotel is worth finding, if you are looking for a pleasant small place to stay in peaceful surroundings. The Petres is almost 1 km from the beach at Kolimbithres, but as it has its own sunny, medium-sized pool this hardly matters. Naoussa, with its bars and restaurants, is only 3 km away and there is a hotel minibus to take you there. The Petres has a pool-side restaurant for those who do not want to cater for themselves, and it serves excellent Greek food.

In style, the Petres mimics the traditional, cubist cottages of the island, with the usual blue-painted woodwork, and there is plenty of greenery, including a scattering of palm trees. White umbrellas and sun loungers surround the pool, and the rooms are simply furnished and adequately serviced. This is not, however, a full-service hotel, and on our most recent visit, on a September afternoon, the staff were conspicuous by their total absence. However, service and facilities are adequate for the price.

~

NEARBY Naoussa; Kolimbithres beach; Parikia.
LOCATION 3 km outside Naoussa, on hillside among fields; car parking
FOOD breakfast, dinner
PRICE ⓔⓔ
ROOMS 16 twin-bedded apartments with WC and shower; all apartments have phone, TV, air conditioning, minibar, kitchen, balcony or verandah
FACILITIES café-bar, sitting rooms, TV room, restaurant, barbecue, airport transfers, swimming pool
CREDIT CARDS MC, V
CHILDREN welcome
DISABLED not suitable
PETS accepted by arrangement
CLOSED Nov-Mar
PROPRIETORS Petres Hotel

CYCLADES

NAOUSSA, PAROS

SWISS HOME
~ ISLAND HOTEL ~

84401 Naoussa, Paros
TEL 0284 51633 **FAX** 0284 52026 **E-MAIL** swissh@otenet.gr

SURROUNDED BY ROCKY HILLS, fields and its own palm trees, the Swiss Home looks rather like a Moroccan kasbah transported to the outskirts of Naoussa, within a few hundred metres of the beach. A family-run hotel, it consists of one two-storey block in Cycladic style, with a large bright restaurant on the ground floor, and some tables on the terrace outside.

The owner's family have more than a century of experience in the hotel industry, having run a hotel in Trabzon in Asia Minor until the 1920s, then operated the Hotel Suisse in Athens before opting for the quieter pace of Paros. Professionalism shows through, but Anna and Marc Polycandriotis are both very friendly and helpful, and there is a real sense that this is a hands-on family business.

The rooms are simple but classically elegant, with tall windows that lead on to balconies, patterned curtains which chime with the bedcovers, and dark-wood antique or reproduction furniture. There is no swimming pool, but the long sandy beach is only a few minutes' walk away. The restaurant, Chez Lucien, serves local dishes, prepared by Anna and her staff. We can recommend this hotel wholeheartedly for comfort, value for money, and a friendly welcome.

NEARBY Kolimbithres beach; Naoussa village; Parikia.
LOCATION 2.5 km from village, 400 m from beach
FOOD breakfast, lunch, dinner
PRICE €€
ROOMS 32; 29 double, 3 suites, all with en-suite WC and bath; all rooms have phone, TV, air conditioning, balcony or verandah
FACILITIES sitting room, bar, breakfast room, restaurant, laundry, minibus service
CREDIT CARDS MC, V
CHILDREN welcome
DISABLED not suitable
PETS accepted by arrangement **CLOSED** Nov-Mar
PROPRIETORS Marc and Anna Polycandriotis

CYCLADES

HIGH MILL HOTEL

~ ISLAND HOTEL ~

84400 Parikia, Paros
TEL 0284 23581 **FAX** 0284 23488

JUST OUTSIDE PARIKIA, the High Mill Hotel is a new building in Parian style. Its square, whitewashed buildings are surrounded by maturing palm trees and gardens, and further landscaping of the surrounding area (which is still rather raw-looking) is planned. The rooms are simple and modern, and there is better than usual attention to detail, with clean towels not only provided daily but laid out neatly pleated on your bed. All rooms have balconies, and most have gorgeous sea views. Furniture is modern, and the en suite bathrooms have miniature tubs as well as showers.

The swimming pool is one level lower than the ground floor, on a terrace surrounded by neat stone walls and well-trimmed grass lawns, and there is a small separate toddlers' pool. The hotel is only 150 metres from the sea, though the coast here is rocky and there is no sandy beach.

The High Mill is only 1 km from Parikia, the island capital, with its restaurants, cafés, nightlife and ferry port. It is also close to the road, and there is some traffic noise during the day and until quite late at night.

~

NEARBY Parikia.
LOCATION 1 km from village, on main road
FOOD breakfast
PRICE €€€
ROOMS 34 double with en suite WC, shower and mini tub; all rooms have air conditioning, verandah, sea view
FACILITIES TV room, breakfast room, garden, swimming pool
CREDIT CARDS MC, V
CHILDREN welcome
DISABLED not suitable
PETS accepted by arrangement
CLOSED Nov-Mar
MANAGER Spyros Maounis

CYCLADES

PARIKIA, PAROS

YRIA HOTEL BUNGALOWS

~ RESORT HOTEL ~

84400 Parikia, Paros
TEL 0284 24154 **FAX** 0284 21167 **E-MAIL** yria1@otenet.gr

THE FIRST IMPRESSION of the Yria is of an oasis of Cycladic buildings in white stucco and exposed masonry, set in a lush garden full of flowers, greenery, palm trees and birdsong. It even smells delicious, with wafts of scent coming from the flowering jasmine. The large reception and lobby bar are bright and breezy, partly opening to the pool terrace and views of the sea. The hotel opened ten years ago, and refurbishment was scheduled in time for the summer 2002 season.

Rooms are a mix of spacious doubles and junior suites, each with its own patio, and are equipped with modern furniture and soft furnishings in muted patterns, predominantly coloured blue and grey. Walls are whitewashed and floors are tiled.

Although the Yria is a large hotel by Parian standards, its village-style layout – it even has its own little blue-roofed, whitewashed chapel, available for weddings – means it does not seem like a big, anonymous hotel, and the staff and management are friendly and service is highly professional. The restaurant, with its stone arches overlooking the pool and surrounding fields, serves reputable Greek and international food, accompanied by wines from the hotel's own vineyard.

~

NEARBY Parikia.
LOCATION 3.5 km from village, near sea; car parking
FOOD breakfast, lunch, dinner
PRICE €€€€
ROOMS 67 twin, 12 junior suites, 1 executive suite, 11 family maisonettes, all with en suite WC and bath; all have phone, TV, air conditioning, minibar, verandah
FACILITIES sitting room, library, restaurant, bar, gym, garden, swimming pool, laundry
CREDIT CARDS MC, V **CHILDREN** welcome
DISABLED access possible **PETS** accepted by arrangement
CLOSED Nov-Mar
PROPRIETORS Hotel Yria

CYCLADES

AIGIALI, AMORGOS

LAKKI VILLAGE

◇ BEACH HOTEL ◇

84008 Aigiali, Amorgos
TEL in season 0285 73253/73505/73506; off season 01 683 1952
FAX in season 0285 73244; off season 01 683 1858

NIKKI GAVALAS REIGNS over this delightful village of rooms, apartments and studios right on the beach at Lakki, among fields and shaded by tamarisk trees. The long beach is sandy, shallow and shelves gently, so is ideal for small children, and the road runs behind the hotel gardens, so there is no traffic. Not surprising, then, that the Lakki Village has a loyal clientele of families who come back almost every year. It has been almost completely rebuilt and refurbished in the last couple of years (and room rates have accordingly doubled), with low-rise one- and two-storey Cycladic cottages surrounding a lush flower and vegetable garden full of sunflowers, tomatoes and courgettes. All the ingredients served in the restaurant are grown (or caught) locally. Rooms are clean and white-washed, with bright blue woodwork, and each has its own entrance and balcony or ground-floor terrace. The restaurant still has very much the feel of an old-time *taverna*, with an array of simmering pots from which you choose your lunch or dinner. Nikki's father, Papa Mihalis, plays his violin most evenings. The only drawback is the local wine, which is harsh even by Cycladic standards. Fortunately, there are bottled alternatives.

◇

NEARBY Lakki beach; Aigiali village; windmills; Hozioviotissa monastery.
LOCATION on the beach, 10 minutes walk from Aigiali village; car parking
FOOD breakfast, lunch, dinner, snacks
PRICE €€€-€€€
ROOMS 10 single, 4 triple, 6 apartments, all with WC and shower; all rooms have phone, radio, kitchenette, balcony or verandah; some rooms are non-smoking
FACILITIES open-air restaurant/bar, garden, beach, shuttle bus to ferry
CREDIT CARDS MC, V
CHILDREN welcome
DISABLED not suitable
PETS accepted
CLOSED Oct-Apr
PROPRIETORS Gavalas family

CYCLADES

FOLEGANDROS

HOTEL KASTRO
~ ISLAND HOTEL ~

84011 Chora, Folegandros
TEL and **FAX** 0286 41230

THE HOTEL KASTRO IS one of our long-standing favourite places to stay in the Cyclades, combining island charm, friendly service, some great views and a fine location in one of the prettiest of archetypal island villages. Wear your sunglasses when approaching the Kastro on a sunny summer day, as it is tucked away in a quiet (even by Chora standards) lane, in a labyrinth of blindingly white plaster walls.

The hotel has been in the hands of the owner's family for some five generations and was refurbished in 1993. The attractive ground-floor breakfast room has massive stone vaulting, which supports the beams and polished boards of the upper floor. Ask for a room with a sea view, and you can gaze out over the Aegean from the steep cliff on which the hotel stands. If you can't get a sea-view room, you can still enjoy the view from the roof terrace. Breakfasts are more generous than in most island hotels, and, for other meals, the restaurants of the village are only a few steps away.

The only drawback is that the nearest beaches are a long hike, but this is unfortunately true of all the hotels in Folegandros, and the Kastro remains our firm favourite on this lovely island.

~

NEARBY Chora.
LOCATION clifftop, on outskirts of village
FOOD breakfast
PRICE €€
ROOMS 12 double and twin
FACILITIES roof terrace
CREDIT CARDS not accepted
CHILDREN accepted
DISABLED no access
PETS not accepted
CLOSED Oct-Apr
PROPRIETOR Despo Danassi-Kallanta

CYCLADES

FIROSTEFANI, SANTORINI

TSITOURAS COLLECTION
~ VILLAGE HOTEL ~

Firostefani, Santorini
TEL 0286 22184 **FAX** 0286 23918 **E-MAIL** tsitouras@otenet.gr

FOR QUIRKY, INDIVIDUAL STYLE, The Tsitouras Collection is hard to beat. Greek businessman Dimitris Tsitouras can take credit for a large share of Santorini's tourism renaissance. His delightful collection of five traditional cave houses around an 18thC mansion at Firostefani, only 700 m from the centre of Thira town, paved the way for a host of style-conscious hotels on the island, and is still among the best. Tsitouras's aesthetic tastes make each of the five houses a unique and eclectic little gallery of art and design, decorated with objects ranging from wind-worn village doors to the iron crowns of Greek Orthodox bishops, ancient pottery, column capitals, icons, 19thC engravings, antique candelabra, printed silks, porcelain and crystal. The bed coverings are pure linen, a lovely luxurious touch, and furnishings are a mix of antique and modern. The House of Nureyev is decorated with sketches of the dancer and fine amphorae and candelabra; the House of Porcelain with fine china plates and Venetian mirrors; the House of the Sea with charts, sea chests and Picasso ceramics; the House of the Winds with icons, marbles, and 18thC engravings; and the House of Portraits with ... portraits. There are superb views. Service is attentive at breakfast time, less so in the afternoon. A pool would make it perfect.

~

NEARBY Thira town; Akrotiri archaeological site; Kameni and Therasia islands.
LOCATION 700 m N of Thira town
FOOD breakfast
PRICE €€€€
ROOMS 5 houses; 1 with double bedroom; 3 with 2 double; 1 with 1 double and 1 single; House of the Winds has 2 double, each with bathroom, and a sitting room and dining room
FACILITIES terrace
CREDIT CARDS MC, V
CHILDREN not suitable **DISABLED** not suitable **PETS** not accepted **CLOSED** Nov-Mar
PROPRIETOR Dimitris Tsitouras

CYCLADES

IMEROVIGLI, SANTORINI

REGINA MARE HOTEL
~ ISLAND HOTEL ~

84700 Imerovigli, Santorini
TEL 0286 25430 FAX 0286 25431 E-MAIL reginamare@otenet.gr

IF YOU WANT A MILLION-DOLLAR view of the sea-filled caldera, volcanic cliffs and nearby islands, and a ringside seat for Santorini's legendary sunsets, all at a price that is modest by Santorini standards, this is the place to choose. The view is equally spectacular from the friendly Regina Mare's pool and the private terraces of each of its rooms. These are in the island style, with vaulted ceilings and platform beds, and are well appointed, with basic cooking facilities: fridge and two electric hotplates. Furniture is simple, as is the familiar whitewash-and-blue-woodwork colour scheme.

At the time of our visit, the bathrooms were showing their age, but the management assured us that they would be modernized over the winter 2001-2 closed season. The hotel attracts a cosmopolitan clientele from Europe, North America and as far away as Australia, and the staff are very helpful and eager to please. The hotel is located some 100 m off the main road at Imerovigli on a steep path (no vehicle access), so it is best to call ahead for help with your luggage. The cafés, restaurants and shops of Thira town are within walking distance, and all the other attractions of the island are a short taxi or bus ride from the hotel.

~

NEARBY Thira town; Akrotiri archaeological site; Oia; Kamari beach.
LOCATION on cliffside at Imerovigli, 1.5 km N of Thira
FOOD breakfast
PRICE €€€€
ROOMS 20 double-bedded studios with en suite WC and shower; all rooms have phone, TV, air conditioning
FACILITIES bar, swimming pool
CREDIT CARDS AE, MC, V
CHILDREN not suitable
DISABLED no access
PETS not accepted
CLOSED mid-Oct to Apr
PROPRIETOR Lefteris Ekonomou

CYCLADES

THIRA, SANTORINI

ENIGMA APARTMENTS

～ VILLAGE APARTMENTS ～

84700 Thira, Santorini
TEL 0286 24024 **FAX** 0286 24023

T HIS FRIENDLY COMPLEX of eight independent apartments is a cut above the usual self-catering complex. Built in 1994, it echoes the typical architecture of Santorini. All the rooms have wooden gallery bedrooms and vaulted ceilings, and each apartment has its own breezy balcony or terrace overlooking the Caldera islands, with breathtaking sunset views. There is also a pretty terrace café. The complex is close to the centre of Thira, Santorini's main town, but is set some distance down the cliffside, giving it some privacy from the often bustling town centre. Call ahead to be greeted and helped with your luggage down the steep stone stairs to reception.

Furniture and decoration are in keeping with the traditional design: expect wooden blanket chests, polished floors, wool rugs and handmade curtains and bedspreads, with old prints, brass lamps and household utensils hanging on the walls. Service is friendly but low-profile: rooms are cleaned daily and towels and linen changed every second day on request, though with an admirably responsible attitude to the environment, you are asked to leave your towels hanging up until they need changing. Breakfast can be served on your own terrace or in the terrace café. Lacking a pool, the Enigma is not quite perfect for sun-worshippers or families.

～

NEARBY Thira town; Akrotiri archaeological site; beaches at Kamari and Perissa; port; Kameni and Therasia islands.
LOCATION cliffside, close to centre of Thira town
FOOD breakfast; room service
PRICE €€€
ROOMS 2 open-plan double studios, 2 loft bedroom apartments with sofa bed on the ground floor, 4 superior 2-bedroom apartments with sofa bed in the living room; all rooms have shower and WC, phone, TV, air-conditioning, hairdrier, safe, basic cooking equipment **FACILITIES** cafe-bar, multilingual reception desk, car and bike rental service **CREDIT CARDS** MC, V
CHILDREN accepted **DISABLED** not suitable **PETS** by arrangement
CLOSED mid-Nov to mid-Mar **PROPRIETORS** K. Ayannis and A. Kondilis

Cyclades

THIRA, SANTORINI

HOMERIC POEMS

↷ VILLAGE APARTMENTS ↶

84700 Thira, Santorini
TEL 0286 24661 **FAX** 0286 24660 **E-MAIL** x-ray-kilo@otenet.gr

A RECENTLY BUILT, ultra-romantic retreat for style-conscious dreamers and honeymooners, Homeric Poems is a small, boutique-style hotel, decorated with quirky flair and perched on a cliff-top terrace at Firostefani, on the outskirts of the island capital.

Twelve large, light apartments open on to sky-high views of the volcanic Caldera islands and are painted in shades of blue, blue-grey and white. Materials are predominantly wood and stone, and colourful island textiles, used for rugs, curtains and bed coverings, soften the look. Each apartment is different from its neighbour, and each is a showcase for the proprietor's eclectic collection of art, antiques and found objects.

It may be stretching a point to claim, as the hotel does, that Thira's sunsets are 'known as the best in the world', but they are certainly up with the best, and Homeric Poems has a splendid location from which to watch them. The fair-sized pool, on a lower cliff-top terrace, also looks out on the magnificent blue bay of the Caldera, the neighbouring islands, and the tiny port far below where the cruise ships and ferries dock. Service here is above average, and the hotel's manager is extremely helpful and knowledgeable.

↷

NEARBY Thira town; Akrotiri archaeological site; beaches at Kamari and Perissa; port; Kameni and Therasia islands.
LOCATION on cliffside at Firostefani, 1 km from centre of Thira town
FOOD breakfast
PRICE €€€€
ROOMS 15 double, triple and quadruple apartments plus honeymoon suite, all with WC and shower; all apartments have phone, TV, air conditioning, minibar, safe, fully equipped kitchenette with fridge, terrace
FACILITIES café bar, pool, laundry service, travel assistance, airport transfers
CREDIT CARDS AE, MC, V **CHILDREN** not suitable **DISABLED** access difficult
PETS accepted by arrangement **CLOSED** Nov-Mar
PROPRIETORS X-Ray Kilo Enterprises

CYCLADES

MEGALOHORI, SANTORINI

VILLA VEDEMA HOTEL

~ LUXURY HOTEL ~

Megalohori, 84700 Santorini
TEL 0286 81797 **FAX** 0286 81798 **E-MAIL** vedema@hol.gr

OPENED IN 1993, the Villa Vedema is the only international luxury chain hotel on Santorini and is a member of the Starwood group's 'Luxury Collection'. Care has been taken, however, to create a hotel with individual style. With only 36 suites, staying at the Vedema feels more like staying in your private villa, and you certainly won't feel that you are in a bland bed-factory. You will, however, be pampered within an inch of your life.

Whitewashed walls, stone floors, shutters on the windows and four-postered brass beds are among the Greek-style features of the rooms, but make no mistake: this is a contender for the title of Greece's most luxurious hotel. Bougainvillea and geraniums add splashes of colour, the pool is magnificent, and there are millionaire touches such as a private beach and an open-air Jacuzzi, as well as an art gallery and jewellery shop. The only possible quibble is over location: set among vineyards, the Vedema doesn't have views to match some less luxurious rivals, nor is it on the sea, though it does offer minibus shuttles to its own stretch of private beach. A choice of restaurants and bars, including a gastronomic restaurant, wine bar, pool-side and Jacuzzi bars, and a private dining room mean that you needn't go out to eat – unusual on Santorini, where few hotels offer full-scale dining. All in all, a place for those in search of a world-class sybaritic holiday with sophisticated service.

NEARBY Thira town; Akrotiri; ancient Kamena and Therasia islands; beaches at Perissa. **LOCATION** 7 km from airport, 6 km from Thira town, 3 km from harbour
FOOD breakfast, lunch, dinner **PRICE** €€€€€
ROOMS 36 apartments and villas for 2, 4 or 6 people
FACILITIES fitness centre, swimming pool, private beach, shops, business and conference centres, helicopter, private jet, limo-service, car and yacht hire, free shuttle to and from airport, port and Thira **CREDIT CARDS** AE, DC, MC, V
CHILDREN welcome **DISABLED** access possible **PETS** accepted by arrangement
CLOSED never
PROPRIETORS Starwood Hotels & Resorts

CYCLADES

OIA, SANTORINI

CALDERA VILLAS

~ VILLAGE HOTEL ~

84702, Oia, Santorini
TEL 0286 71285 **FAX** 0286 71425

A MILLION-DOLLAR VIEW of the Caldera islands and glittering bay is one of the prime reasons for staying in this attractive collection of cliff-edge villa rooms which tunnel, in traditional Santorinian fashion, into the soft rock of the island. The Caldera extends several levels down from the main street, and each of its nine rooms has a small terrace, just big enough for a café table and two chairs and the perfect place for breakfast or sunset drinks. In the midday sun, the Caldera can be dazzling, as its rooms are painted the traditional white of the Cyclades, with immaculate bright blue woodwork. Clumps of bougainvillea add splashes of scarlet to this blue and white colour scheme.

Inside, rooms are pleasantly cool and shady, simply furnished and minimally decorated. The pool is tiny but pretty, and, like the rooms, it has a fantastic panoramic view, as does the café and breakfast area. The sets of stairs which connect the various levels make this hotel unsuitable for people with disabilities, and although children are accepted, it is not ideal for families. For couples seeking a romantic retreat, however, there are few better places.

Rooms and public areas are spotless, but service, especially during mid-afternoon siesta, could be more attentive.

~

NEARBY Oia; Caldera islands; Amoudi.
LOCATION cliffside, Oia village
FOOD breakfast
PRICE €€€
ROOMS 9 double
FACILITIES café, swimming pool
CREDIT CARDS not accepted
CHILDREN accepted
DISABLED not suitable **PETS** accepted by arrangement
CLOSED never
PROPRIETORS Caldera Villas SA

CYCLADES

OIA, SANTORINI

CANAVES

~ VILLAGE HOTEL ~

84702 Oia, Santorini
TEL 0286 71453 **FAX** 0286 71195 **E-MAIL** canaves@otenet.gr

THIS COMPLEX OF 24 HOUSES on the edge of Oia village is very nearly a village in its own right. Whitewashed stone steps wind between the blue-painted arched doorways, leading from street level to the terrace and pool. Canaves I and II are two groups of traditional houses built into the rock. The houses vary in size from cosy studio apartments for couples to larger two- and three-bedroom villa suites sleeping up to six. Each has its own private terrace overlooking the volcanic lagoon, several hundred metres below.

All the houses are air-conditioned and all are authentically decorated with traditional antique furniture and local island handicrafts such as prints, pottery and local textiles.

Each house has a living area, one or two comfortable bedrooms, and a fully equipped kitchen including refrigerator and oven, a bath or shower and direct telephone. The pool is one of the most striking in Oia, and is designed so that it seems to vanish into its own cool cave in the cliffside, and there is a pleasant pool bar. Service is friendly, and more professional than in some rival properties: room service is available in theory, but you should not expect it to be up to the standards of a big city hotel. Off-street car parking is an added bonus; car hire and excursions can be arrranged.

~

NEARBY Oia village; Thira town; Kameni and Therasia islands; Akrotiri archaeological site; Amoudi beach; Kamari and Perissa beaches
LOCATION 800 m from village centre, 12 km from Thira; car parking
FOOD breakfast, snacks; room service
PRICE ©©©
ROOMS 24 with WC and shower; all rooms have phone, air conditioning, minibar, kitchen
FACILITIES bar, swimming pool, car hire, excursions
CREDIT CARDS MC, V **CHILDREN** accepted
DISABLED not suitable **PETS** accepted **CLOSED** Nov-Mar
MANAGER Ioannis Haidemenos

CYCLADES

OIA, SANTORINI

ESPERAS TRADITIONAL HOUSES

~ ISLAND HOTEL ~

84702 Oia, Santorini
TEL 0286 71088 **FAX** 0286 71613 **E-MAIL** esperas@otenet.gr

T O CALL THESE RESTORED cave-houses and apartments 'traditional' is
stretching a point, since few islanders in bygone decades enjoyed luxuries such as a turquoise swimming pool with its own bar. Only five minutes
from the centre of Oia, the Esperas looks out over the Aegean and the
island of Therasia, and a few hundred metres below is the tiny fishing harbour and miniature beach at Amoudi. Exposed stonework and fired earth
tiles make a change from the relentless, dazzling white stucco of most Oia
buildings, and there is a fine sunbathing terrace.

Rooms are imaginatively designed and furnished, with traditional-style
wooden sofas upholstered in pastel patterns, whitewashed walls, blue
woodwork, indirect lighting and tiled floors in mellow ochre and terracotta. Attractive touches include old earthenware amphoras filled with dried
flowers.

In some apartments, the bed is on a wooden gallery reached by a steep,
wooden stair-ladder. The rooms are spacious, and each of the larger honeymoon suites has a proper, full-length bathtub with a whirlpool – a rarity
on most Greek islands.

~

NEARBY Amoudi beach and fishing harbour; Oia village; Thira town; Akrotiri
archaeological site; Kamari beach.
LOCATION on the cliffside at Oia
FOOD breakfast
PRICE €€€
ROOMS 15 1 and 2 bedroom units, all with en suite WC and shower; all have
phone, TV, air conditioning
FACILITIES bar, internet, swimming pool
CREDIT CARDS MC, V
CHILDREN not suitable
DISABLED no access **PETS** not accepted
CLOSED mid-Oct to Apr
PROPRIETORS Esperas SA

CYCLADES

OIA, SANTORINI

HOTEL MUSEUM
~ VILLAGE MANSION HOTEL ~

84702 Oia, Santorini
TEL 0286 71515 **FAX** 0286 71516

THIS ELEGANT LITTLE HOTEL on Oia's (pedestrian) main street has an interesting history and plenty of style and atmosphere. With its central location, it is more user-friendly for the less energetic than some of the village's cliffside guesthouses, which require a steep walk. During the 19th century, when Oia was the most important village on Santorini, the great grandfather of the present proprietor was the British consul and this was the village's loveliest mansion. King Othon and Queen Amalia slept here, and it is still the grandest place to stay in Oia. Damaged by the 1956 earthquake, it later became a museum (hence the name) and was restored as a hotel during the 1990s. Bedrooms are decorated with paintings by prominent Greek artists and each of the nine apartments is furnished with handmade, individual furniture and equipped with colour TV, radio, minibar and complete kitchen. Most apartments have terraces with west-facing views from which to admire the sunset, and the upper apartment has panoramic views of the whole spectacular island. The small garden swimming pool is decorated with frescoes inspired by those found at ancient Akrotiri, and the proprietor claims that the two olive trees which shade the pool-side bar are the oldest on the island. Moreover, there are two suites available for guests who seek luxury.

~

NEARBY Thira; beaches at Perissa and Kamari; Akrotiri archaeological site; volcanic island of Nea Kameni.
LOCATION centre of Oia village, N tip of Santorini
FOOD breakfast
PRICE €€€
ROOMS 9; 7 double with WC and shower, 2 luxury suites; all rooms have TV, minibar, kitchenette
FACILITIES café-terrace, garden, swimming pool
CREDIT CARDS MC, V **CHILDREN** not suitable **DISABLED** not suitable **PETS** accepted
CLOSED never
PROPRIETOR Hotel Museum SA

CYCLADES

OIA, SANTORINI

OIA VILLAGE HOTEL

~ VILLAGE HOTEL ~

84702 Oia, Santorini
TEL and **FAX** 0286 71114

GERMAN-BORN WRITER Nina Keller-Roditi has spent years transforming the 23 once-derelict cave-houses into a delightfully peaceful place to stay, with fabulous views over the caldera. They now make an enchanting hotel just outside Santorini's prettiest village. However, in Oia, perched 300 metres above a lagoon created by a titanic explosion some 4,500 years ago, fabulous views are taken for granted, and it is the proprietor's personal welcome that makes the Oia village special.

Most of the accommodation is in the unique Santorinian tunnel houses, each of which has been restored and individually furnished and decorated, though the proprietor's taste tends towards the chintzy. Some of the rooms are in more modern additions which have been designed to blend in seamlessly. Typical touches include vaulted ceilings and walled beds, and although rooms are pleasantly cool, they are also light and airy, with giddy views from each window and terrace. Breakfast here is above the usual standard in Greece, with plenty of fresh fruit, juice and yoghurt, served on your own terrace or by the pool, which, like the rooms, has a view that can hold you spellbound. The restaurants, shops and cafés of Oia village are only 5 to 10 minutes' walk away.

~

NEARBY Oia village; Thira town; Kameni and Therasia islands; Akrotiri archaeological site; Amoudi beach; Kamari and Perissa beaches.
LOCATION 800 m south of Oia village centre, on cliff top
FOOD breakfast, snacks
PRICE ©©©
ROOMS 23 houses with double living /bedroom or with separate bedroom, fully equipped kitchen or kitchenette, bathroom, minibar, terrace
FACILITIES pool, snack bar, laundry, safe deposit, reception can arrange excursions, boat trips, car hire
CREDIT CARDS V **CHILDREN** accepted **DISABLED** not suitable **PETS** not accepted
CLOSED Nov-Mar
PROPRIETOR Nina Keller-Roditi

CYCLADES

PIRGOS, SANTORINI

ZANNOS MELATHRON HOTEL
∼ MANSION HOTEL ∼

84701 Pirgos, Santorini
TEL 0286 28220 FAX 01 0286 28229 WEBSITE www.zannos.gr

THIS RECENT NEWCOMER to the Santorini hotel scene is set within a 19thC mansion built by Michael Zannos, one of the wealthiest islanders of that era, master of this property, and of an adjoining Renaissance villa built in 1750. Hidden away in the middle of a picturesque village, with panoramic views of the island, this is perhaps the most sophisticated hotel on Santorini.

'Melathron' in Greek means 'palatial mansion', and that is a fair description of the Zannos, which has been styled by one of Greece's leading designers, Yannis Tseklenis, with ten eclectically decorated suites set around a maze of stairs and miniature courtyards. All are equipped with designer furniture, fabrics, linens, china and silver, and are furnished with fine antiques, bearing the names of Zannos family members through the decades.

Service is by far the best on Santorini, with just the right mix of unobtrusive attentiveness, and the restaurant lives up to the rest of the property. The Zannos strives for old-world elegance, but complementing its *salons* filled with antiques and original works of art are modern facilities including ISDN internet access, fax, e-mail and voice-mail. In short, it is the perfect place for the discerning high-flier looking for luxurious relaxation, and no other Santorini hotel can really compete.

NEARBY vineyards; historic villages; crater and islands; Akrotiri archaeological site; Perissa beach; Thira town.
LOCATION Pirgos village centre, 3.5 km from Thira town and 2 km from ferry port
FOOD breakfast, lunch, dinner; room service
PRICE €€€€
ROOMS 10; 7 1-bedroom suites, 3 2-bedroom suites, all with en suite bathroom, shower, phone, satellite TV, air conditioning
FACILITIES restaurants, wine bar, terrace bar, courtyards, swimming pool
CREDIT CARDS AE, DC, MC, V CHILDREN accepted
DISABLED access possible PETS by arrangement CLOSED never
PROPRIETORS Hotel Enterprises Vardis SA

DODECANESE

GIALOS, SYMI

HOTEL ALIKI

∼ VILLAGE HOTEL ∼

Akti G. Gennimata, 85600 Symi
TEL 0241 71665 **FAX** 0241 71655 **E-MAIL** info@simi-hotelaliki.gr

TWO STEPS FROM THE SEA, in a peaceful spot just around the corner from the Gialos harbour area, this pretty hotel was converted from a neoclassical sea-captain's house dating from 1895. It was one of the first of the new wave of 'boutique hotels' in Greece and is now first class and very well run. The outside is painted in primrose yellow, with a large wrought-iron balcony across the front of the building. Tall, shuttered windows make the bedrooms light and airy, but the hotel also has air conditioning for really hot weather. Refurbished in 1999, it has polished wood floors and period furniture and many of its guests come back every summer. Rooms have en suite showers, and it is worth asking for a balcony or sea view, as some rooms at the back and side of the hotel are quite small.

There is a large, breezy sitting room, bar and reception area on the ground floor, and breakfast is much more lavish than in some island hotels. On the quayside opposite the front door there are half a dozen umbrella-shaded café tables, and if you fancy a dip but don't want to travel 15 minutes by car to the nearest beach, there is a bathing ladder bolted to the wall of the harbour, where the water is very clean.

∼

NEARBY Gialos harbour; beach at Pedi; Panormitis monastery.
LOCATION Gialos waterfront
FOOD breakfast
PRICE €€€
ROOMS 15; 12 double and twin, 3 suites, all with en suite WC and shower; all rooms have phone, radio, air conditioning
FACILITIES sitting room, bar
CREDIT CARDS MC, V
CHILDREN accepted
DISABLED not suitable
PETS accepted by arrangement
CLOSED Nov-Apr
PROPRIETOR Giorgios Kypraios

DODECANESE

GIALOS, SYMI

LES CATHERINETTES
~ VILLAGE HOTEL ~

85600 Symi
TEL and **FAX** 0241 72698

THIS IS ONE OF THE MOST CHARMING little hotels in the Greek islands. Overlooking the perfect natural harbour from which streets of pretty houses rise steeply, Les Catherinettes is a four-storey, neoclassical building, decorated in pink stucco and with wrought-iron balconies on each floor. There's a bustling, cavernous *taverna* on the ground floor, and the tiny reception is on the floor above, reached by a narrow flight of steps. Inside, polished wood stairs with blue-painted banisters lead to the upper floors, where the high, cool and airy rooms have ceilings painted in elaborate floral and abstract patterns. They have tall windows and balconies overlooking the harbour. You can sit on your balcony looking down at the day trippers arriving on the excursion boats from Rhodes, smug in the knowledge that they'll be gone in a few hours, and you will have this delightful small town all to yourself. Les Catherinettes is one of the longest-established hotels on the island – during the Second World War it was the headquarters of the Italian occupation forces, and the Italian commander signed his surrender in the restaurant downstairs. It is efficiently run by friendly proprietor Julie and her daughter Marina. With its steep stairs, upstairs rooms and location on a busy quayside street it is perhaps less than ideal for families with babies or toddlers.

~

NEARBY beaches; Panormitis monastery; Rhodes island
LOCATION on the harbour, beaches 10 minutes by bus
FOOD breakfast, lunch, dinner, snacks
PRICE €€
ROOMS 10; 6 twin, 4 studios with kitchenette
FACILITIES taverna
CREDIT CARDS not accepted
CHILDREN not suitable
DISABLED not suitable **PETS** not accepted
CLOSED never
PROPRIETOR Julie Arvanitis

DODECANESE

HOTEL CAVA D'ORO

~ TOWN HOUSE HOTEL ~

Kisthinou 17, 85100 Rhodes
TEL 0241 36980 **FAX** 0241 77332

THIS 800-YEAR-OLD BUILDING within the medieval city walls is one of only a handful of hotels that stand out in the stunning Old Town, perhaps the best preserved medieval city in Europe. Although it was the residence of the commander of the Italian garrison during the Italian occupation of the Dodecanese from 1912 to 1945, he must have been a man of untypically modest tastes.

Converted into a small hotel in 1987, the Cava d'Oro has no 'grand hotel' atmosphere. Rooms are cosy, simply decorated but quiet and comfortable, and there is a small, shaded courtyard where breakfast is served and you can have drinks during the day. The harbour and sights of the Old Town are just a few minutes' walk, but the nearest beach is on the opposite side of the New Town area, too far away to be within convenient walking distance. Service is perhaps best described as low profile. The hotel enjoyed a moment of modest fame when it was visited by ex-Monty Python and globetrotter Michael Palin and a TV crew during the filming of Palin's *Pole to Pole* . Although tucked away in a hard-to-find back street, the hotel is easily accessible by car or taxi, unlike most in the Old Town area. It is also very reasonably priced, especially by the larcenous standards of Rhodes.

~

NEARBY Old Town; archaeological museum; Palace of the Grand Masters; harbour.
LOCATION within the walls of the medieval town
FOOD breakfast
PRICE ⓔ
ROOMS 13 with en suite WC and shower; all rooms have phone, air conditioning
FACILITIES courtyard garden
CREDIT CARDS not accepted
CHILDREN not suitable
DISABLED not suitable
PETS not accepted
CLOSED Nov-Mar
PROPRIETOR Athanasios Mavrakis

CYCLADES

AGIOS IOANNIS, MIKONOS

APOLLONIA BAY HOTEL
~ LUXURY RESORT HOTEL ~

84600 Agios Ioannis, Mikonos
TEL 0289 27890 **FAX** 0289 27641

EVEN WITH SO MANY STRONG competitors on the island, the newly opened five-star Apollonia Bay must be considered one of the best hotels on Mikonos. It impresses immediately with its style and character. The friendly staff are all dressed in white, and the hotel appears to have a higher staff-to-guest ratio than most – or perhaps it is just that they are more attentive. The open-plan bar-reception area is bright and breezy, opening on to an elegant restaurant terrace with tables under an awning or in the sun. The terrace overlooks a large, turquoise pool, which has views out to sea, over the beach (only two minutes' walk away) and a tiny fishing harbour, with the once sacred island of Delos on the horizon. Sun loungers and thatched parasols surround it, and stone terraces, covered with maturing shrubs, rise in tiers behind the pool. The spacious rooms, built in a variation on the traditional village design, are connected by stone paths, stairs and miniature squares overflowing with greenery. They are unfussily decorated, with tiled floors, and attractively furnished with reproductions of 19thC furniture in the style found in well-off Greek homes of the period; the junior suites have four-poster beds. All the rooms have a sea-view balcony.

~

NEARBY Agios Stefanos beach; Chora; Ornos beach.
LOCATION Agios Ioannis, 3.5 km from Chora; car parking
FOOD breakfast, lunch, dinner, snacks; room service
PRICE ©©©©
ROOMS 31; 27 double, 1 suite, 3 mini-suites, all with en suite bath; all rooms have phone, TV, video, air conditioning, minibar, hairdrier, balcony
FACILITIES restaurant, snack bar, gym, sauna, swimming pool, pool bar, laundry
CREDIT CARDS AE, MC, V
CHILDREN welcome
DISABLED not suitable
PETS accepted by arangement
CLOSED Nov-Mar
PROPRIETORS Apollonia Bay Hotel SA

CYCLADES

CAVO TAGOO, MIKONOS

HOTEL CAVO TAGOO
~ RESORT HOTEL ~

84600 Cavo Tagoo, Mikonos
Tel 0289 23692 **Fax** 0289 24923 **E-MAIL** cavotagoo@hol.gr

THIS AWARD WINNING hotel is reminiscent of a real Cycladic village, with its tiers of whitewashed houses rising among granite cliffs and boulders, artfully worked into the landscaping. The view is splendid, gazing out over the bright blue bay, and the rooms surround an equally bright blue pool. Some of the rooms are too close to the occasionally busy coast road for perfection (as is the pool); so ask for a room in one of the upper buildings, which have a better view and no traffic noise.

It is easy enough to build a hotel which pastiches the Cycladic style on the outside, and in fact most Mikonos hotels do. The Cavo Tagoo, however, meticulously carries this theme through into the bedrooms, with flagstone floors, wooden galleries, beds with wrought-iron frames or on wooden platforms, and striped blue and turquoise coverlets. Arched niches in the stonework, or brightly-painted dressers, display colourful china plates or old pottery vases, and in some rooms the rocks against which the hotel is built form part of the design.

The hotel is a delightful place at sunset, and dinner in the candlelit, poolside restaurant is a treat. Service is courteous and professional.

~

NEARBY Chora; island beaches; Delos.
LOCATION 1 km from Chora, above main road; car parking
FOOD breakfast, lunch, dinner; room service
PRICE €€€€
ROOMS 72; 67 double, 5 suites; all rooms have phone, TV, video, air conditioning, minibar, balcony or terrace, sea view
FACILITIES sitting room, TV room, restaurant, shop, swimming pool, pool bar, laundry
CREDIT CARDS AE, MC, V
CHILDREN accepted
DISABLED not suitable
PETS not accepted
CLOSED Oct to mid-Apr
PROPRIETORS Aegean Coasts SA

CYCLADES

ORNOS, MIKONOS

KIVOTOS CLUBHOTEL

~ LUXURY RESORT HOTEL ~

84600 Ornos, Mikonos
TEL 0289 24094 **FAX** 0289 22844

HIDING ITS GLAMOUR behind a high granite wall, the Kivotos Clubhotel is undoubtedly the most exclusive and luxurious hotel on the island.

Stone arched terraces surround a pair of glorious swimming pools and descend in steps to the sea and a tiny private beach, while behind and around them rise white Cycladic cottages, each with a wooden balcony or terrace, dazzling white plaster and blue shutters. These simple exteriors conceal a wealth of stylish interior touches, including antique or reproduction wooden furniture, dazzling white, beautifully crisp bed linen, vaulted ceilings and doorways and many other details which artfully blend the traditional style of the islands with modern luxury. Throughout the complex, there are sculptures, fragments of contemporary art, mosaics and frescoes created by local craftsmen and internationally-known artists.

Kivotos combines the feel of a small, family-run hotel with all the elegance and comforts of a luxury villa. Service levels are very high, and two gourmet restaurants, La Meduse and Mare, offer wonderful menus with influences from all over the world. For a taste of gastronomic Greece, there is the traditional taverna, Le Pirate.

~

NEARBY Ornos; Chora.
LOCATION W side of Ornos bay, 3 km from Chora; car parking
FOOD breakfast, lunch, dinner, snacks,
PRICE ©©©©©
ROOMS 45 double and suites, all with en suite bath; all rooms have phone, TV, air conditioning, minibar, safe; satellite video and fax on request
FACILITIES billiard room, 4 restaurants, internet cafe, 2 bars, fitness centre, squash court, massage, sauna, Jacuzzi, cinema, drugstore, 2 swimming pools (1 seawater), private beach, laundry, private yacht, shuttle to airport and ferry port
CREDIT CARDS AE, DC, MC, V **CHILDREN** accepted
DISABLED not suitable **PETS** accepted by arrangement
CLOSED Nov-Mar
PROPRIETORS Sp Michopoulos SA

CYCLADES

ORNOS, MIKONOS

SANTA MARINA

~ LUXURY RESORT HOTEL ~

84600 Ornos Bay, Mikonos
TEL 0289 23220 **FAX** 0289 23412 **E-MAIL** info@santamarina.gr

THIS WELL-DESIGNED member of one of the world's leading luxury hotel groups is a recent arrival on the Mikonos scene. The Santa Marina is aware of its reputation for exclusivity, and has gate security to ensure guests' privacy and safety. More than most Mikonos hotels, the Santa Marina straddles the line between business and pleasure (it has substantial business and meeting facilities) and, in comparison with the relaxed dress code of most island hotels, it comes as a surprise to encounter formally dressed reception staff.

The emphasis throughout is on classic style. Rooms and suites, with their marble tiled floors, have neutral coloured walls, but sunny yellow and vivid blue cushions, curtains and other soft furnishings. The villas, with their white, traditional-style wood-ceilinged sitting rooms, large sofas, cane armchairs and private pools that are bigger than the main pool in some hotels, are outstanding.

To complete the picture, the Santa Marina has that rare thing in Greece, a private beach: a crescent of white pebbles with sun loungers and thatched umbrellas, accessible only from the hotel. Two restaurants offer a wide range of menus, from classic Greek to nouvelle Mediterranean and Asian dishes.

~

NEARBY Ornos; Chora; island beaches.
LOCATION E side of Ornos bay, 3 km from Chora
FOOD breakfast, lunch, dinner, snacks; room service
PRICE €€€€€
ROOMS 90; 64 rooms, 23 suites, 3 villas with private pool, 2 restaurants, 2 bars
FACILITIES health club, beauty centre, swimming pool, private beach, 2 tennis courts
CREDIT CARDS AE, DC, MC, V
CHILDREN welcome
DISABLED access possible
PETS accepted by arrangement **CLOSED** Nov-Mar
PROPRIETOR Starwood Hotels & Resorts

CYCLADES

PSAROU, MIKONOS

GRECOTEL MYKONOS BLU

~ LUXURY RESORT HOTEL ~

84600 Psarou, Mikonos
TEL 0289 27900 **FAX** 0289 27783
E-MAIL sales@ath.grecotel.gr

THE MYKONOS BLU is undeniably a chain hotel, but equally undeniably an exceptionally stylish one. It earns its place in this guide partly on location – between two beautiful blue bays – but mainly on imaginative decoration, fine service standards, and attention to detail. Blue is the theme throughout, from the blue marble of the reception desk and the modern paintings which adorn the bright lobby sitting area through to the paintwork and soft furnishings of the rooms. The glass brandy barrels, filled with bright blue dye, which are ranked behind the reception desk are a strikingly original decorative touch, and in the bathrooms, blue-painted wooden ceilings make a change from the relentless use of marble in so many Greek hotels.

Although this is a large resort, it does not feel overwhelming, as rooms are arranged village-style, in tiers around the headland. White umbrellas and a stone-paved terrace surround a two-tier pool, and for those who prefer sea-bathing or tanning on the beach, the hotel has its own ranks of umbrellas and sun loungers on the sand, reached by a stone staircase.

The Delos sitting rooms, with their white linen sofas and white-shaded lights, are delightful. The remarkable sculptured bar, a circle of polished metal, looks like something out of a science-fiction movie, but still manages to blend in with the rest. This hotel is highly recommended for those looking for a full-service resort hotel of outstanding style.

~

NEARBY Ornos beach; Chora.
LOCATION on headland above Psarou beach
FOOD breakfast, lunch, dinner
PRICE €€€€
ROOMS 102; 92 double, 10 junior suites with private pool, all with en suite WC and shower; all rooms have phone, TV, air conditioning, balcony, terrace
FACILITIES sitting rooms, 2 restaurants, 2 bars, fitness centre, outdoor swimming pool, indoor swimming pool, beach **CREDIT CARDS** AE, MC, V **CHILDREN** welcome
DISABLED not suitable **PETS** accepted by arrangement **CLOSED** mid-Oct to May
PROPRIETORS Grecotel SA

DODECANESE

OLD TOWN, RHODES

SAN NIKOLIS HOTEL
~ TOWN HOUSE HOTEL AND APARTMENTS ~

61 Hippodamou, 85100 Rhodes
TEL 0241 34561 **FAX** 0241 32034

THIS PRETTY STONE BUILDING, draped in bougainvillea, stands just inside the high medieval battlements of the Old Town. Steeped in romantic history, the main building features two medieval arched rooms, and overlooks the ruins of the ancient Roman market. Potted palm trees growing by the entrance add to its semi-tropical appearance, and inside, more trees shade an attractive courtyard. Owner Nikolis Sotiris and his Danish wife Mariana have turned the San Nikolis into one of the Old Town's most sought-after places to stay, so book well ahead. Nikolis spends every winter adding period touches to the hotel, such as the canopied beds which can be found in many of the rooms.

The San Nikolis also has a full-service restaurant offering lunch and dinner; breakfast is served on the roof terrace, which has marvellous views over the Old Town's tiled roofs to the harbour. The bar serves a wide range of drinks and cocktails, and there is a snug with an original, 800-year-old fireplace – hardly in demand in summer, but cosy in winter.

~

NEARBY medieval fortifications; Palace of the Grand Masters; archaeological museum; harbour.
LOCATION 300 m from harbour in the Old Town
FOOD breakfast, lunch, dinner
PRICE €€€
ROOMS 20; 12 double, 8 suites, all with en suite WC and shower; some rooms have verandah or balcony
FACILITIES bar, restaurant, roof terrace, courtyard
CREDIT CARDS AE, MC, V
CHILDREN accepted
DISABLED not suitable
PETS not suitable
CLOSED never
PROPRIETORS Nikolis and Mariana Sotiris

CYCLADES

CHORA, ANDROS

HOTEL EGLI
TOWN HOTEL

84500 Chora, Andros

TEL 0282 22303
FAX 0282 22159
FOOD breakfast
PRICE €€
CLOSED Nov-Mar
PROPRIETORS Antonis and Christiana Valmas

OWNED BY ANTONIS and Christiana Valmas, who also own the new Stageira, this old-fashioned hotel beside the church square in Chora, Andros's main town, will appeal to anyone with a taste for nostalgia. The Egli is an elegant, neoclassical mansion, with pale yellow walls detailed in white, wrought-iron balconies, and tall shuttered windows. It looks out over the palm trees and fountain of the square, and its handful of café tables are on wide steps connecting the church with the street below. This is for pedestrians only, so the hotel is free of traffic noise. Inside, its 15 high-ceilinged rooms are reached by a very steep, narrow, winding wooden stair and have tall windows with shutters and very basic furnishings.. The hotel has a certain quirky character, but some may find it expensive.

CHORA, MIKONOS

ALEFKANDRA KITCHEN
TOWN RESTAURANT

84600 Chora, Mikonos

TEL 0289 224504
PRICE €€€
CREDIT CARDS MC, V
CLOSED Nov-Mar

THE ALEFKANDRA KITCHEN is unashamedly a tourist restaurant which trots out the familiar mullet, squid, grilled fish and salad, but it can hardly be faulted: it offers simple food and a picturesque setting. It stands next to the sea, with views of the famous windmills, and beside the tiny Catholic chapel, a landmark of Chora's so-called 'Little Venice'. Outdoor tables with red and white cloths and wooden chairs are grouped under a vast awning (the restaurant occupies most of the square). Doomed lobsters lurk in tanks beside the kitchen. Service is friendly in an impersonal sort of way, and brisker than in many Chora eating places. Choose it for the location and a reasonably priced seafood dinner, not for an imaginative menu, and you won't be disappointed.

CYCLADES

CHORA, MIKONOS

DILES
TOWN RESTAURANT

Lakka Square, 84600 Mikonos

TEL 0289 22120
PRICE €€€
CREDIT CARDS MC, V
CLOSED lunch, Nov-Mar

THIS RESTAURANT, semi-enclosed beneath a canopy beside the pool of a holiday apartment complex, has a high reputation and is certainly a cut above the average Chora restaurant with its imaginative à la carte choices. Its impressive wine list includes some of the new breed of quality Greek wines as well as imports. You could easily run up a hefty bill here, as the array of white linen and sparkling glasses indicates as soon as you step inside. Fortunately, Diles also offers a set menu which is remarkable value, with home-baked bread, creative starters such as cheese and hazelnut soufflé, main courses such as grilled sea bream or pork in mustard sauce, salad and dessert. Service (as in most Mikonos restaurants) is sadly indifferent.

CHORA, MIKONOS

TAVERNA NIKOS
TOWN TAVERNA

Plateia Agias Monis, Chora

TEL 0289 24320
PRICE €€
CREDIT CARDS not accepted
CLOSED Nov-Mar

ON A STONE-PAVED square beside a tiny red-domed monastery church, with tables inside and outside, Nikos is one of the best traditional *tavernas* in Chora and offers excellent value for money.

All the traditional favourites, such as *kleftiko* and lamb with lemon, are served and there is a wide range of non-meat dishes for vegetarians, including a dish of the day. Nikos's casserole dishes are very filling, and definitely a choice for a large dinner, not a light lunch. This unassuming *taverna* is a welcome alternative to the other sometimes pretentious and often over-priced restaurants of Mikonos.

CYCLADES

FIROSTEFANI, SANTORINI

SUNROCKS
VILLAGE APARTMENTS

Firostefani, Santorini

TEL 0286 23241
FAX 0286 23991
FOOD breakfast
PRICE €€
CLOSED Nov-Mar
PROPRIETORS Sunrocks

THE APPROPRIATELY NAMED SUNROCKS, which basks in the Aegean sunshine on the cliffs at Firostefani on the outskirts of Thira town, recently expanded from 15 rooms to 26 and elevated itself from B class (the Greek equivalent of four-star) to A class (five-star), a grading it deserves not only for location and facilities but for its helpful staff. Like so many Thira hotels, it has awesome views over the sea. There are three types of room, all with sea views. The pool, though tiny, has a panoramic view too. Breakfast is served at the pool side, and for those who intend to make full use of the kitchenette for self-catering there's a grocery delivery service. Access is by a long flight of cobbled steps, so tell the hotel your arrival time so they can help with luggage.

IMEROVIGLI, SANTORINI

CHROMATA
CLIFF-SIDE APARTMENTS

Imerovigli, 84700 Santorini

TEL 0286 24850
FAX 0286 23278
FOOD breakfast
PRICE €€€
CLOSED Nov-Mar
PROPRIETORS Chromata SA

THIS TRADITIONAL COMPLEX of apartments is partly tunnelled into the cliffside in true Santorinian fashion, and even the imaginatively-designed pool partly vanishes into a cool, shady grotto. Service is attentive, with helpful, multilingual reception staff (who are on duty until midnight, much later than in most small island hotels); and there's 24-hour room service, which isn't found in all Santorini's smaller hotels. Furnishings are a tasteful mix of traditional and modern, and the view of the Caldera is as good as any on the island. Breakfast, an American-style buffet, reflects a strong U.S. clientele and is more substantial than in many rival properties.

CYCLADES

IMEROVIGLI, SANTORINI

HOTEL HELIOTOPOS

TOWN HOTEL

Imerovigli, 84700 Santorini

TEL 0286 23670
FAX 0286 23672
E-MAIL helio@otenet.gr
FOOD breakfast, snacks
PRICE €€€
CLOSED Nov-Mar
PROPRIETORS Heliotopos SA

PERCHED LIKE A SWALLOW'S NEST on the cliffs just outside the centre of Thira, the island capital, Heliotopos is a sybarite's hideaway. Typical of its relaxed quality is the fact that breakfast is served from 08.30 until 13.30, and is not just coffee, croissants and juice but a full buffet of island specialities, including the hotel's own home-baked bread. A typical Santorini cellar, carved out of the lava rock, makes a cool and shady bar. Heliotopos is a collection of one- and two-storey traditional buildings with vaulted roofs, built on old foundations, and in a quiet part of the village. Most of the rooms have sleeping galleries above the living space, as well as a double or twin bedroom, and all have at least one private balcony looking out over the volcanic Caldera far below.

MESSARIA, SANTORINI

ARCHONTIKO ARGYROU

TOWN APARTMENTS

84700 Messaria, Santorini

TEL 0286 31669
FAX 0286 33064
FOOD none
PRICE €€€
CLOSED Nov-Mar
PROPRIETOR Angeliki Argyrou

THIS DIGNIFIED, neoclassical mansion with its pink and white stucco exterior was built in 1888 by Santorinian landowner and winemaker Georgios Argyros, and is still in the hands of the Argyros family. There are two comfortable guest apartments on the ground floor, while the family home on the first floor is a treasury of local heritage in the shape of frescoes, 19thC furniture, paintings and art objects; it can be visited by arrangement. The apartments have access to a private courtyard, but there is no pool. There is a (limited) maid service, so this is self-catering accommodation in the truest sense. The shops, bars and restaurants of Thira are about 1500 metres away; Kamari beach takes around 30 minutes by foot.

CYCLADES

OIA, SANTORINI

AETHRIO HOTEL
VILLAGE HOTEL

84702 Oia, Santorini

TEL 0286 71040 **FAX** 0286 71930
WEBSITE www.greek-
tourism.gr/aethrio-hotel
FOOD breakfast
PRICE €€€
CLOSED Nov-Mar
PROPRIETORS Damigos Family

THIS HOTEL STANDS (literally) head and shoulders above all its local competitors. Located at almost the highest point of the village, it has the best and biggest pool in Oia, and has a panorama over the roofs of the village towards the Caldera and west for one of the finest sunset views on an island famed for them. Designed as a village within a village, the Aethrio is an attractive clutter of traditional vaulted cottages, linked by flagstoned pathways. Apparently the original building, which now houses the restaurant, reception, and a light, low-ceilinged sitting room, was originally a knitwear factory; some of the original machinery is still in place – an unusual conversation piece. White canvas umbrellas and blue tin café tables stand round the pool. Rooms are bright, simple and elegant.

OIA, SANTORINI

OIA MARE VILLAS
VILLAGE HOTEL

84702 Oia, Santorini

TEL and **FAX** 0286 71070/71881
FOOD breakfast
PRICE €€€
CLOSED Nov-Mar
PROPRIETORS Oia Mare Villas

BALANCED ON THE CLIFFS which overlook the Caldera of Santorini, this is one of the most magnificently sited and romantic places to stay in all Greece. Designed in a style which echoes that of a traditional Santorini village, the suites are painted dazzling white and are simply but elegantly furnished, and look down over a fabulous, bright blue pool with a bar and terrace. Should you tire of the pool, there is a tiny beach at the foot of the cliff on which the Oia Mare stands, reached by a steep, wide stair (you can do it the easy way by hiring a donkey). Although the beach is pebbly, the water is deliciously clean, and there are several excellent small fish restaurants beside the miniature harbour of Amoudi. Accommodation is in two-bedroom, one-bedroom or studio apartments.

CYCLADES

PERIVOLAS
VILLAGE HOTEL

84702 Oia, Santorini

TEL 0286 71308 FAX 0286 71309
Athens office: TEL and FAX 01 620
8249

FOOD breakfast
PRICE €€€
CLOSED Nov-Apr
PROPRIETOR Konstantinos Psyhas

FACING STRONG LOCAL competition, this group of first-class traditional houses is possibly the best place to stay in Oia, on Santorini... and maybe in the Cyclades. The buildings, converted from the old village winery, ooze local character. Facing southwest from its cliff-top site, Perivolas has a miraculous view of Santorini's legendary sunrises and sunsets. The rooms are large and airy, with vaulted ceilings and alcoves, simply whitewashed walls, and beautiful hand-crafted furnishings such as hardwood chests and teak steamer chairs, colourful rugs and floor cushions. The pool is larger than most of the Oia hotel pools, and the pool-side terrace is delightful at any time of day. There is plenty of greenery, too, to soften the stark but beautiful surroundings, and the staff are helpful and friendly.

1800
TOWN RESTAURANT

84702 Oia, Santorini

TEL 0286 71485
PRICE €€€€€
CLOSED Nov-Mar
CREDIT CARDS AE, MC, V

IN SANTORINI'S BEST RESTAURANT, the focus is on creative Mediterranean cooking, served in elegant surroundings, with pure white linen, sparkling glassware and attentive service. The wine list is extensive and includes some of the island's best wines as well as quality vintages from elsewhere in Greece. The menu includes a cosmopolitan range of traditional dishes, such as barley soup with yogurt and mint or Mesolonghi caviar with buckwheat pancakes. The main courses are mainly meat, with the emphasis on veal, though duck, lamb and chicken are on the menu too. There are also fish dishes, with the catch of the day served simply grilled. 1800 is not cheap, but could be the perfect place to dine on your last night.

DODECANESE

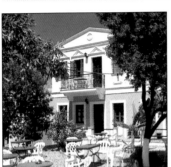

OPERA HOUSE

TOWN GUESTHOUSE

85600 Gialos, Symi

TEL 0241 72034
FAX 0241 72035
FOOD self-catering
PRICE €€
CLOSED Nov-Mar
PROPRIETOR Manolis Minorakis

ALTHOUGH RECENTLY BUILT, this collection of blue-and-white-painted, neo-classical-style buildings merges with the traditional Simiot mansions in the older parts of the pretty harbour town. Set among shady trees in maturing gardens about 150 m inland, accommodation is in cool, airy studios, each of which has a large kitchen and functional bathroom. All are traditionally furnished with wooden sofas and colourful striped rugs. It's quiet, friendly, and owner-managed by a local family who spent many years in Sydney, Australia (hence the name of the hotel). There is an outdoor bar, where cold drinks are served during the day, and the many harbourside restaurants and bars are only a five-minute stroll away.

CRETE

AREA INTRODUCTION

Greece's largest island is a destination in its own right, a country within a country, with a distinctive culture and history (before uniting with Greece in 1913 it was even, briefly, an autonomous republic). Close to 200 km from west to east and up to 80 km wide, it is an island of dramatic landscapes, with harsh mountains (snow capped in spring) rising above some of Greece's best beaches and fertile coastal plains. There are large package holiday resorts along the north coast (forming an almost continuous tourism ghetto east of Iraklio) but Crete is large enough to absorb many visitors and offer plenty of alternatives.

Iraklio, the capital, is a rather gritty and characterless modern town and lacks hotels of distinction, but two historic harbour towns, each surrounding a Venetian fortress, more than make up for this. Crete was a Venetian possesssion from the 13th until the mid-17th century (it was the birthplace of El Greco, one of many exiles from the island after the Turkish conquest) and, in the old quarters of Rethymno and Chania we discovered a number of charming small hotels, mostly in old Venetian town houses.

Also worthy of mention, we decided, were several of the better hotels in and around the Elounda and Agios Nikolaos areas, in eastern Crete. These are primarily self-contained resort hotels, set in attractive gardens and with a degree of flair, charm and luxury that sets them apart from the run of the mill holiday resorts. While larger than most of the hotels in this book, they are of low-rise, village-style design and retain a 'small hotel' atmosphere.

Finally, outside the towns and away from the beaches, there are a number of uniquely Cretan village properties in restored and (minimally) modernized traditional farming and mountain settlements. These allow you to experience a little of the full flavour of village life, and will appeal to those who want littlemore than peace, quiet, beautiful surroundings and a good book.

Lying well south of the rest of Europe, Crete has hot sunshine as early as April (and a brief and dazzlingly colourful wildflower spring) and as late as October, and some of the hotelslisted here stay open year round. That said, the best times to visit are definitely Easter to mid-June and September to the end of October, and those with a low tolerance for high temperatures should avoid the almost African heat of July and August.

WESTERN CRETE

MILIA VILLAGE

~ TRADITIONAL VILLAGE ~

73012 Milia, Vlatos, Crete
TEL 0822 51569

MILIA IS UNIQUE, and only for those who relish a simple, ecologically correct existence. The 'village' is a painstaking recreation of Crete's not-so-distant past: the Tsourounakis and Makrakis families offer 13 rooms in traditional houses rebuilt between 1982 and 1993 in local stone and wood, and furnished and decorated in the manner of Crete in past decades. There are two communal dining and sitting rooms and there are beautiful views of the mountains of Crete's wild west from the stone porches of each house. All the buildings stand on the original foundations of the village. The kitchen doubles as a reception area and has a phone for emergencies – one of the few aspects of modern life that touches Milia. Each room is different, but all are equipped only with basic furnishings and decorated with household objects that have been lovingly collected. There is no electricity in the rooms – heating is provided by wood-burning cast-iron stoves – water comes from two mountain springs, and large central boilers heated by wood fires provide hot water. In summer, lighting is powered by solar panels, but in winter a generator provides electricity in the evenings. Breakfast, lunch and dinner are served in the communal dining room; you can make your own tea and coffee.

~

NEARBY White Mountains; Vlatos village; west coast
LOCATION 55 km SW of Chania, 4.5 km from Vlatos village
FOOD breakfast, lunch, dinner
PRICE €
ROOMS 13 double and twin
FACILITIES sitting room, dining room, garden
CREDIT CARDS not accepted
CHILDREN welcome
DISABLED not suitable
PETS welcome
CLOSED never
PROPRIETORS I. Tsourounakis and E. Makrakis

WESTERN CRETE

CHANIA

AMPHORA HOTEL

~ TOWN HOUSE HOTEL ~

Parados Theotokopolou 20, 73100 Chania, Crete
TEL 0821 93224 **FAX** 0821 93226

THIS 13TH-14THC MANSION HOUSE in Venetian-Turkish style is in the heart of the characterful old quarter of Chania, literally a stone's throw from the harbour. The roof-top terrace and some rooms offer great views of the Venetian harbour and the old fortress opposite, the tiled rooftops of the old town, and the White Mountains inland – perhaps the best view in Chania, some guests reckon.

Public areas and bedrooms are decorated and furnished in traditional Cretan style, with patterned wool rugs and old clay amphorae, polished wooden floors and high panelled ceilings. The colour scheme is soft pink, with blue woodwork. Breakfast is more imaginative and substantial than usual, with an excellent European-American buffet. The à la carte restaurant is one of the best places in town to sample real Cretan cooking.

The Amphora would be perfect were it not for the numerous reports that this otherwise charming hotel is very noisy in summer ('use earplugs' suggests one disgruntled ex-guest), because it is so close to the many harbour-side cafés and a loud disco downstairs. The walls between rooms are thin, too. The Amphora is probably at its best outside peak season, when most of the harbour-side cafés, and the downstairs disco, are closed.

~

NEARBY Archaeological museum; market; Venetian fortress; harbour; White Mountains.
LOCATION Chania old quarter, next to harbour
FOOD buffet breakfast, lunch, dinner
PRICE €€
ROOMS 20 double (extra bed on request), all withWC and shower; all rooms have phone, central heating; 3 have kitchenette; 2-bedroom apartments
FACILITIES restaurant, roof terrace
CREDIT CARDS MC, V
CHILDREN accepted **DISABLED** not suitable **PETS** not accepted **CLOSED** never
PROPRIETOR Mr Stelios Tsourounakis

WESTERN CRETE

CHANIA

CASA DELFINO
~ TOWN HOUSE HOTEL ~

Theofanous 9, 73100 Chania, Crete
TEL 0821 84700 **FAX** 0821 96500

AN AIR OF GRANDEUR SURROUNDS the Casa Delfino, from its Venetian-style courtyard with fountain and mosaics secluded behind decorative wrought-iron gates to its marble floors and decorative antiques. It's quite the most exclusive address in Chania, set within a 17thC Venetian mansion that has been restored with an eye for luxury. That said, the Casa Delfino is not snooty: the atmosphere is informal and the staff are friendly and helpful. It is close to the busy harbourside, but set back in a quiet alley so it doesn't suffer from noise pollution at night, and it has fine roof-top views over the castle, the old quarter, and the mountains beyond. The suites are extremely luxurious and are individually designed, with separate living and sleeping areas; the colour scheme, in creamy hues that echo the marble public areas and exterior, is neutral. Facilities are up to the minute – dataports and modem connections are available, but unfortunately there is no swimming pool.

~

NEARBY Archaeological museum; market; Venetian fortress; harbour; White Mountains.
LOCATION Chania old quarter, next to harbour
FOOD breakfast, lunch, dinner
PRICE €€€€
ROOMS 16 suites with WC and shower (some with Jacuzzi tubs); all rooms have phone, TV, air conditioning, minibar or kitchenette, hairdrier
FACILITIES courtyard bar
CREDIT CARDS MC, V
CHILDREN accepted
DISABLED access difficult
PETS accepted
CLOSED never
PROPRIETOR Manthos Markantonakis

WESTERN CRETE

NOSTOS

~ TOWN GUESTHOUSE ~

42-46 Zambeliou, 73113 Chania, Crete
TEL 0821 94743 **FAX** 0821 54502

PRETTILY PAINTED IN EYE-CATCHING BLUE, pink and yellow, Nostos offers one of the friendliest welcomes in Chania. So it should: 'nostos' means 'homecoming' in Greek. Located on a narrow, pedestrian street in the heart of the old town, little café tables and rush-seat chairs make the exterior look like an archetypal Greek picture postcard, and pots of flowers dangle from the first-floor windows.

The studio rooms have gallery beds and balconies with fine views of the castle, the harbour and the mountains, and Nostos is set far enough back from the harbour to escape the worst of the night-time noise from bars and restaurants, though those taking a room with a harbour view will hear some.

The building is about 600 years old, and the owner has incorporated parts of an early Venetian church and a Turkish bath, winning an award for applied architecture in the process. The pretty roof-top terrace, shaded by honeysuckle and vines, is a pleasant place in which to escape the afternoon heat. Service is friendly, but minimal – it's clean and tidy, but this isn't for people expecting a full-service hotel.

~

NEARBY harbour; fortress; market; archaeological museum; beach.
LOCATION in the middle of the old harbour area
FOOD breakfast, snacks
PRICE €€
ROOMS 12 apartments with gallery bedroom plus sofa bed, all with kitchenette, shower and WC, phone, 2 with open fireplace, 2 with harbour view
FACILITIES roof terrace, café-bar, fax
CREDIT CARDS MC, V
CHILDREN not recommended
DISABLED not suitable
PETS not accepted
CLOSED Nov-Mar
PROPRIETOR Ioannis Orfanoudakis

WESTERN CRETE

PALAZZO RIMONDI

~ TOWN HOUSE HOTEL ~

21 Xanthoudidou and 16 Har. Trikoupi, 74100 Rethymno, Crete
TEL 0831 51289 **FAX** 0831 51013 **E-MAIL** rimondi@otenet.gr

THE PALAZZO RIMONDI is tucked away in an arcaded courtyard, with walls painted in pretty shades of rose and ochre, behind arched, wrought-iron gates.

Vaulted roofs, carved stone, panelled wood ceilings and wooden oriels looking out on to the pretty café courtyard are the keynotes of this superbly restored complex of 15thC buildings, recently restored by its architect owners and undoubtedly one of the most luxurious and exclusive hideaways in Rethymno. The Rimondi is charming, not least because of a very pleasant courtyard with a breakfast café and swimming pool (with a special area for children) and pretty terraces.

Traditional Cretan specialities are served at breakfast. All the apartments have a sitting room, sleeping area and dining area, and most of them have attractive original features such as stone carved arches, wooden ceilings and wooden oriel windows that look out over the courtyard or the surrounding rooftops. The owners have achieved an excellent balance between old and new, retaining the building's character without trying too hard to achieve a medieval look throughout – despite their medieval stonework, the bedrooms are stylishly modern with some traditional influences, such as low benches along each wall, and tiled floors.

~

NEARBY Venetian fortress; Rimondi fountain; Church of St Francis; markets; town beaches
LOCATION in the old quarter of Rethymno
FOOD breakfast, snacks
PRICE €€€€
ROOMS 20 double apartments
FACILITIES TV/video room, café-bar, courtyard, swimming pool
CREDIT CARDS MC, V
CHILDREN welcome
DISABLED access difficult
CLOSED never
PROPRIETORS Touristiki Rethymno SA

WESTERN CRETE

VENETO SUITES AND STUDIOS

~ TOWN HOUSE HOTEL ~

4 Epimenidou, 74100 Rethymno, Crete
TEL 0831 56634 FAX 0831 56635 E-MAIL info@veneto.gr

GOTHIC ARCHES, massive exposed oak beams and stonework, mellow marble and polished wood floors set the scene in this lovely 15thC Venetian *palazzo* with a vivid history, lovingly restored by its present owners. The oldest part of the building was originally a 15thC monastery. In the 16th century it was rebuilt as the *loggia* of the Venetian officers who commanded Rethymno's forbidding *fortezza*. In the 19th century it was the home of a wealthy Turkish pasha, and after the liberation of Crete in 1913 it was given by the Greek government to the grandfather of the present owner, a hero of the war against the Turks. Its most recent restoration was in 1997. Rooms are a mix of large (50 square metres) suites and studios. The restaurant is well worth a visit, serving the best of Greek and Mediterranean cuisine, and there is a pretty walled garden with three fountains, built around the wells which were the original water supply.

A wide range of additional services, including massage and sauna, adds to the general air of luxury, and service (which includes room service) is courteous and attentive. All in all, one of the best places in Crete for a self-indulgent stay, and although the Veneto does not have a pool of its own, it is only a short walk from Rethymno's town beach, and half an hour's drive from the uncrowded beaches of the west.

~

NEARBY town beach; markets; *fortezza*; historic mosque
LOCATION in old quarter of Rethymno
FOOD breakfast, dinner; room service
PRICE €€€
ROOMS 10; 5 suites with separate sleeping area and sitting room, 5 studios, all with shower; all rooms have phone, TV, air conditioning, safe, kitchenette and fridge, balcony or terrace
FACILITIES TV room, bars, snack bar, restaurant, sauna, garden
CREDIT CARDS MC, V **CHILDREN** accepted
DISABLED access difficult
PETS accepted **CLOSED** never
MANAGER Ioannis Prokopakis

EASTERN CRETE

ELOUNDA BEACH HOTEL
∼ LUXURY RESORT ∼

Elounda Beach, 72053 Elounda, Crete
TEL 0841 41412 **FAX** 0841 41373 **E-MAIL** elohotel@eloundabeach.gr

THE CONCIERGE DESK OFFERS LIMOUSINE, helicopter and executive jet charter service as well as yacht hire, a fair indication of the Elounda Beach's pretensions. For an unbeatable combination of world-class luxury and privacy, stay in one of 25 utterly sybaritic suites with heated pools, which form a 'millionaire's village' within this superb resort. Undoubtedly one of the world's best hotels, the Elounda Beach is no midget – it has 215 de luxe suites and villas – but its low-rise, village-style layout (complete with art gallery and Cretan art museum, boutiques and a chapel) means it does not feel like a large package holiday resort. Appealing to a cosmopolitan, multi-national clientele, it is close to the sports facilities of the beautiful, pine-covered Elounda peninsula and stands in its own lush, tropical-seeming grounds. The hotel has a wide variety of sports and activities, including five tennis courts, volleyball and the full array of water sports from scuba diving to water skiing. Particularly suitable for families, the Elounda Beach has its own semi-private beaches with umbrellas and sunbeds, a children's playground and a supervised programme of activities for kids. The only possible criticism is that you will not want to leave the resort to see the rest of Crete.

∼

NEARBY Spinalonga; Agios Nikolaos; Lasithi
LOCATION Elounda peninsula, 10 km N of Agios Nikolaos
FOOD breakfast, lunch, dinner, snacks; 24-hour room service
PRICE €€€€€€
ROOMS 215 de luxe suites and villas; all have phone, TV, video, CD player, air conditioning, minibar, safe, Jacuzzi, twice daily housekeeping; 25 suites have heated pools
FACILITIES 4 restaurants, sushi bar, café, 3 bars, shops, gym, sauna, beauty parlour, beach beds, sea-water pool, garden, tennis, volleyball
CREDIT CARDS AE, MC, V **CHILDREN** welcome **DISABLED** suitable
PETS accepted
CLOSED Nov-Mar
PROPRIETORS Ilios SA

EASTERN CRETE

KOUTSOUNARI, IERAPETRA

KOUTSOUNARI NAKOU VILLAGE

~ SELF-CATERING VILLAGE ~

PO Box 31 72200 Ierapetra, Crete
TEL 0842 61291 **FAX** 0842 61292

THIS HOLIDAY VILLAGE on a hillside above the Libyan Sea offers the best of both worlds – choose to stay in one of the original stone-built cottages which were restored in the 1970s (with the addition of modern kitchens and bathrooms); or in the modern A Class bungalows of the adjoining Nakou Village, part of the same complex.

All the original cottages have a verandah (book early for one with a sea view) and most have a tiny garden, usually full of sunflowers and geraniums. The Nakou Village bungalows all have large verandahs with splendid views over the surrounding olive groves and down to the sea. Nakou also has a pool (which guests at the Koutsounari cottages can use) and the long sandy beach is a not-too-tiring 1,200 m walk.

There is a snack bar, and the Kyraleni taverna owned by Dora Mandalas next to the site offers tasty Cretan and Cypriot dishes. This is very much a village-style resort for those who are happy to cater for themselves, and you will need to rent a car. Koutsounari gets top marks for facilities, but is not a full-service hotel with such frills as room service or a choice of restaurants.

~

NEARBY beach; Ierapetra.
LOCATION 9 km from Ierapetra; car parking
FOOD snacks, taverna next door
PRICE €€
ROOMS 17 traditional stone 1 and 2 bedroom cottages, 16 modern 1 and 2 bedroom apartments and studios
FACILITIES snack bar, swimming pool
CREDIT CARDS MC, V
CHILDREN welcome
DISABLED access possible
PETS accepted
CLOSED Koutsounari Nov-Mar
MANAGER Emmanolis Mandalas

WESTERN CRETE

CHANIA

VILLA ANDROMEDA

TOWN HOUSE HOTEL

*150 Eleftherios Venizelou, 73133
Chania, Crete*

TEL 0821 28300 **FAX** 0821 28300
E-MAIL vilandro@otenet.gr
FOOD snacks
PRICE €€€
CLOSED never
PROPRIETORS Nefeli SA

I**T'S THE SWIMMING POOL** that impresses many guests at this neoclassical mansion, built in 1870 and lovingly restored. Palm trees on the terrace, and a lushly planted garden, lend a tropical touch, and the pool itself is prettily tiled in a mosaic of turquoise and deep blue. The Andromeda was once the German consulate building, and it still has some lovely original features which are typical of the grand mansions of the district at the turn of the 19th century, including elaborate painted ceilings, white marble floors, fine staircases and many balconies. The pool has been unobtrusively squeezed in behind the original building. Service is friendly and efficient as far as it goes, but it's assumed that guests will take full advantage of the self-catering facilities in each suite.

CHANIA

DOMA HOTEL

TOWN HOUSE HOTEL

*124 Eleftherios Venizelou,
Halepa, Chania*

TEL 0821 51772
FAX 0821 41578
FOOD breakfast, lunch, dinner
PRICE €€€€
CLOSED never
PROPRIETORS Rena Valiraki and
Ioanna Koutsoudaki

T**HIS NEOCLASSICAL MANSION** in Chania's Halepa seafront quarter was built a century ago as the Austrian consulate and (briefly, in 1940) was also the British consulate. It has been a hotel since the early 1970s and although the original old front has some period charm, the overall impression from the outside is rather functional (not aided by its location behind a busy coastal highway, nor by the inelegant top storey which was clumsily added some decades ago). Inside it's a different matter, with friendly staff and public areas decorated with an eclectic collection of antiques and curios including family photographs and a collection of traditional headgear from all over the world. Rooms are comfortable, but not memorable.

WESTERN CRETE

CHANIA

CASA LEONE

TOWN HOUSE HOTEL

Parodos Theotokopolou 18, Akti Koundouriotou, Chania

TEL and **FAX** 0821 76762
FOOD breakfast
PRICE €€€ **CLOSED** never
PROPRIETORS Casa Leone Hotel SA

B UILT ALMOST SIX CENTURIES AGO, the 'House of the Lion' was once a Venetian mansion (taking its name from Venice's heraldic beast, the Lion of St Mark) and has been restored by its present owners with meticulous attention to period detail. Indirect lighting, polished wood floors, Venetian mirrors and antique and reproduction furniture make this among the grandest places to stay in Chania. Another period feature is the courtyard with its fountain, and the Casa Leone also has an almost intimidatingly smart cocktail bar which wouldn't be out of place in an up-market hotel in Athens. At the west end of the waterfront, this is a great place to stay, marred only by some noise from the harbour restaurants in high season.

CHANIA

SUITES PANDORA

TOWN HOTEL

Lithinon 29 73100 Chania, Crete

TEL 0821 43589
FAX 0821 57864
WEBSITE www.pandorahotel.gr
FOOD breakfast
PRICE €€
CLOSED Nov–Mar
PROPRIETORS Pandora SA

S ET HIGH ABOVE THE HARBOUR and looking down over the old town, Suites Pandora is a stylish property, originally built in 1870 and since refurbished into a collection of two- and four-bed suites surrounding a secluded courtyard. Some face inward over this inner court, others look out to sea, and all have the high ceilings, balconies and tall shuttered windows typical of 19thC neoclassical architecture.

A shared terrace looks out over the harbour and offers great views. As with several other properties in the area, the assumption seems to be that guests will be mainly catering for themselves: service is limited to breakfast, basic reception, cleaning and linen change – this isn't a full-service hotel.

W ESTERN C RETE

M YTHOS S UITES

T OWN HOUSE HOTEL

*12 Plateia Karaoli, 74100
Rethymno, Crete*

T EL 0831 53917 **F AX** 0831 51036
E-MAIL info@mythos-crete.gr
Food breakfast
P RICE €€
C LOSED never
P ROPRIETOR Nadia Paraski

T HIS 16THC V ENETIAN MANSION (actually two old Venetian buildings knocked into one around a courtyard with a tiny but pretty swimming pool) is on a quiet back street in the picturesque old part of Rethymno, but within easy walking distance of the beaches, harbour, cafes, restaurants and sights of the city. The owner, Nadia Paraski, has restored the building with painstaking attention to detail since the mid-1990s. Arched doorways give access to a sunny courtyard. Rooms on the upper floors have private wooden balconies, while those surrounding the pool have verandahs adjoining the courtyard. All studios and suites are furnished with pretty traditional furniture, and imaginative use has been made of original features.

V ECCHIO H OTEL A PARTMENTS

A PARTMENT HOTEL

4 Daliani, 74100 Rethymno

T EL 0831 54985 **F AX** 0831 54986
E-MAIL vecchio@otenet.gr
Food buffet breakfast, snacks
P RICE €€ **C LOSED** Oct-Apr
P ROPRIETORS Vecchio Hotel
Apartments SA

N OT MUCH REMAINS to indicate that these very attractive apartments (used by a number of European holiday companies) were originally Venetian mansions. The hotel is a complex of two buildings, with a mix of hotel rooms (usually available only off-peak) and studios (more readily available to individual clients). Ideal for a longer stay, and excellent value, the Vecchio is set in a quiet street in the heart of the old quarter; the building is mainly new, but is painted in pale blue and terracotta to match its medieval surroundings. The pool is great, much bigger than any in the old town area, a real bonus. Rooms are simple, modern, well equipped and attractively decorated. A peaceful place, with no traffic or restaurant noise, and a useful base for exploring Western Crete.

EASTERN CRETE

PLAKA, ELOUNDA

SPINALONGA VILLAGE
SELF-CATERING VILLAGE

72053 Elounda, Crete

TEL and **FAX** 0841 41494/6
FOOD breakfast
PRICE €€€€ **CLOSED** Nov-Mar
PROPRIETORS Kentavros SA

ONLY 50 M FROM THE BEACH, the Spinalonga Village is a perfect base for couples or families. Cottages are built in local stone, each standing on its own terrace, planted with flowers and shrubs. You will need a car if you plan to explore (there is a useful off-road car park behind the cottages), but there are shops and eating places nearby at Plaka village (an 800 m walk). The plutocratic resort area of Elounda, with its sports facilities, is only 4 km away.

The Spinalonga looks out over the Gulf of Mirabello and takes its name from the Venetian fortress-island which commands the approaches to the Gulf and the pretty little port of Agios Nikolaos, not far away.

AGIOS NIKOLAOS

MINOS BEACH ART 'OTEL
LUXURY RESORT

72100 Agios Nikolaos, Crete

TEL 0841 22345 **FAX** 0841 22548
E-MAIL info-minos@mamhotel.gr
FOOD breakfast, lunch, dinner, snacks; room service
PRICE €€€€€
CLOSED Nov-Mar
PROPRIETORS Tourist Enterprises Agiou Nikolaou SA

THIS MEDIUM-SIZED RESORT, with its splendid views of the Gulf of Mirabello, is set in tranquil, flower-filled gardens and a has a reputation for excellent service and fine food – which it lives up to. Only 1 km from the centre of the popular resort and harbour town of Agios Nikolaos, the hotel is nevertheless very peaceful, and has a couple of small sandy beaches and several rocky inlets which are as private as it is possble for a beach in Greece to be. Choose between garden- and sea-view rooms (all have balconies, but book early if you must have a sea view). The most expensive accommodation is in bungalows with direct access to the beach.

EASTERN CRETE

ASPROS POTAMOS

TRADITIONAL VILLAGE HOUSES

72231 Ierapetra, Crete

TEL and **Fax** 0843 51694
FOOD self catering
PRICE €€
CLOSED Nov-Mar
PROPRIETORS Aleka Halkia

ONLY FOR REAL LOVERS of the simple life, this little settlement of old-fashioned cottages has no modern conveniences. Drinking water comes from the well and lighting is by paraffin lamp (though bathroom lights and fridges in each house run off solar electricity). Inside, the cottages have stone floors, ceilings made of calamus reed in the traditional way, wooden furniture, and striped wool cushions and blankets. If this sounds a little Spartan in its simplicity, it is, but the complete lack of 21stC gadgets is wonderfully relaxing once you get used to it. Truly a great escape; ideal for the overstressed city-dweller. However, if you feel the need for some excitement, there are dozens of bars and tavernas spread out along the beach and road through Makrigialos.

WHITE RIVER COTTAGES

TRADITIONAL VILLAGE HOUSES

72231 Ierapetra, Crete

TEL and **Fax** 0843 51120
FOOD self catering, taverns nearby at Makrigialos
PRICE €€€
CLOSED Nov-Mar
PROPRIETORS Elma SA

TAKING ITS NAME from the nearby valley (Aspros Potamos means 'White River'), this very attractive little group of traditional shepherds' cottages, with whitewashed walls, stone-flagged floors, low wooden ceilings and corner fireplace nooks, stands in groves of pine, olive and carob trees. Simple and delightful, it is one of the better examples of restored vernacular architecture in this part of the island.

The long sandy beach at Makrigialos is less than 2 km away, and the cottages are surrounded by flowers and greenery. In these traditional surroundings the pretty little swimming pool comes as a welcome surprise.

Hotel & Restaurant Names

Hotels are arranged in order of the most distinctive part of their name. Other unusual parts of the name, such as 'Archontiko' (mansion), 'Casa', 'Pirgos' (tower), 'Taverna' (restaurant) 'Ta' and 'To', 'Villa', 'Xenonas' (guesthouse) are also given. Common prefixes, such as 'Guesthouse', 'Hotel' or 'Pension' have been omitted

Hotel & Restaurant Names

HOTEL & RESTAURANT NAMES

Hotel & Restaurant Names

Hotel & Restaurant Names

O

P

R

S

Hotel & Restaurant Names

LOCATIONS

In this index, hotels and restaurants are arranged by the name of the city, town or village they are in or near. Where a hotel is in a very small place, it may be indexed under a nearby place which is more easily found on maps. Where a hotel is one of the many island villages named 'Chora', or where placenames are duplicated elsewhere, the name of the island or district is also given (in brackets).

A

B

C

LOCATIONS

D

E

F

G

LOCATIONS

LOCATIONS

LOCATIONS

LOCATIONS

SPECIAL OFFERS

Buy your *Charming Small Hotel Guide* by post directly from the publisher and you'll get a worthwhile discount. *

Titles available:	Retail price	Discount price
Austria	£9.99	£8.50
Britain	£10.99	£9.50
Britain's Most Distinctive Bed & Breakfasts	£9.99	£8.50
France	£11.99	£10.50
France: Bed & Breakfast	£9.99	£8.50
Germany	£9.99	£8.50
Ireland	£9.99	£8.50
Italy	£11.99	£10.50
Mallorca, Menorca & Ibiza	£9.99	£8.50
Paris	£10.99	£9.50
Southern France	£10.99	£9.50
Spain	£9.99	£8.50
Switzerland	£9.99	£8.50
Tuscany & Umbria	£9.99	£8.50
USA: Florida	£9.99	£8.50
USA: New England	£9.99	£8.50
Venice and North-East Italy	£9.99	£8.50

Please send your order to:

Book Sales,

Duncan Petersen Publishing Ltd,

31 Ceylon Road, London W14 OPY

enclosing: 1) the title you require and number of copies

2) your name and address

3) your cheque made out to:

Duncan Petersen Publishing Ltd

*Offer applies to this edition and to UK only.

VISIT DUNCAN PETERSEN'S TRAVEL WEBSITE AT
www.charmingsmallhotels.co.uk
• Research interesting places to stay • Online book ordering –special discounts • Room booking service

SPECIAL OFFERS

If you like *Charming Small Hotel Guides* you'll also enjoy
Duncan Petersen's *Versatile Guides/Travel Planner &
Guides*: outstanding all-purpose travel guides written by
authors, not by committee.

Titles available:	Retail price	Discount price
Australia Travel Planner & Guide	£12.99	£10.50
California The Versatile Guide	£12.99	£10.50
Central Italy The Versatile Guide	£12.99	£10.50
England & Wales Walks Planner & Guide	£12.99	£10.50
Florida Travel Planner & Guide	£12.99	£10.50
France Travel Planner & Guide	£12.99	£10.50
Greece The Versatile Guide	£12.99	£10.50
Italy Travel Planner & Guide	£12.99	£10.50
Spain The Versatile Guide	£12.99	£10.50
Thailand The Versatile Guide	£12.99	£10.50
Turkey The Versatile Guide	£12.99	£10.50

Travelling by car? Duncan Petersen's *Backroads* driving guides
include original routes and tours – avoid the motorways and main
roads and explore the real country. Full colour easy to read
mapping; recommended restaurants and local specialities;
practical advice on where to stop, visit and picnic.

Titles available:	Retail price	Discount price
Britain on Backroads	£9.99	£8.50
France on Backroads	£9.99	£8.50
Italy on Backroads	£9.99	£8.50
Spain on Backroads	£9.99	£8.50

Please send your order to:

Book Sales,

Duncan Petersen Publishing Ltd,

31 Ceylon Road, London W14 OPY

enclosing: 1) title you require and number of copies

2) your name and address

3) your cheque made out to:

Duncan Petersen Publishing Ltd

*Offer applies applies to this edition and to UK only.